GO AND PLAY

GOLF

GO AND PLAY

GOLF

TECHNIQUES

TONY JACKLIN
AND PETER DOBEREINER

ILLUSTRATIONS BY CHRIS PERFECT

STANLEY PAUL

LONDON

FOR MICHAEL

Stanley Paul & Co. Ltd

An imprint of Random Century Group

20 Vauxhall Bridge Road, London SW1V 2SA

Random Century Australia (Pty) Ltd
20 Alfred Street, Milsons Point, Sydney 2061

Random Century New Zealand Limited
18 Poland Road, Glenfield, Auckland

Century Hutchinson South Africa (Pty) Ltd
PO Box 337, Bergvlei 2012, South Africa

First published as *Jacklin's Golf Secrets* 1983
This edition 1992

Copyright © Tony Jacklin and Peter Dobereiner
1983, 1992
Illustrations © Stanley Paul & Co. Ltd 1983

The right of Tony Jacklin and Peter Dobereiner to
be identified as the authors of this work has been
asserted by them in accordance with the Copyright, Designs and Patents Act, 1988

Set in Garamond Light by SX Composing Ltd
Printed and bound in Great Britain by Clays Ltd
A catalogue record for this book is available from
the British Library

ISBN 0 09 177203 6

Photographic acknowledgement: The authors and
publishers would like to thank Phil Sheldon for
supplying all the photographs in this book.

CONTENTS

PREFACE

Most golf instruction books carry a strong implication that if the reader will diligently apply himself to learning a thousand or more specific and disjointed actions, down to such detail as varying the pressure of individual fingers on the grip, and then perform them in the correct sequence and at the correct speed, he will become as good a player as the illustrious author.

This book implies no such claim. For one thing, it is impossible to learn golf by reading about the correct tension of the left pinkie at the top of the backswing. For another thing, although this book might set someone on the long road to becoming a champion, it is statistically unlikely. Consider the odds. Less than one person in a thousand who takes up golf becomes accomplished enough to turn professional. And less than one professional in a thousand becomes accomplished enough to win a championship. That makes the odds 1,000,000 to one. No book can confer the gifts of rare talent, physique, dedication and opportunity to beat those odds.

Besides, not too many people want to become champions. There is more, much more, to golf than winning championships, thank goodness. Golf is mainly a recreational exercise, the best one in the world of sport, played for enjoyment by people who are either unable or unwilling to spare much time for it. The aim of this book is to allow every golfer, from beginner to scratch player, to develop his or her game to the fullest potential of his or her individual circumstances.

Now, all those 'his and hers' are clumsy and so, for the sake of simplicity, from now on masculine pronouns only will be used. This is not to imply any male chauvinist piggery, simply a device to circumvent a regrettable gap in the English language. So female readers are assured that, in the absence of suitable dual purpose pronouns, they are warmly embraced by the authors whenever the words 'he', 'him' or 'his' are employed.

In the same way, no slight is

intended to left-handers of either gender by the fact that all the instructions are given on the basis of right-handed golf. Please accept this brief exhortation as both an apology and a request to transpose right for left whenever appropriate.

There are well over ten thousand muscular responses during a golf swing, each related and co-ordinated with the others. The swing lasts slightly more than one second, during which time it is humanly possible to have two thoughts, possibly three if you think quickly. It is therefore quite impossible for anyone to monitor every movement of every muscle as the swing is being made. What we can all do very easily is recall the feeling of everyday actions, such as cutting down a tree, whipping a top, leading a child across the road and twirling a conker on a string. By the time a person reaches the age of ten he or she knows perfectly well how to play golf because all the game requires us to do is to reproduce movements with which we are all familiar and which we perform without any conscious thought or difficulty.

The purpose of this book is to teach the game of golf by marshalling those experiences and applying them to the business of playing golf. Several scientists have studied golf and have concluded that it is physically impossible for a human being to control such forces and speeds to the fine tolerance needed to hit a ball long and straight. Well, everyone else knows that it is possible. What's more it is easy. You already have a good swing: the purpose of this book is to enable you to bring it out and put it to work on the golf course. Do not be dismayed by anything you may have read or heard about the myriad intricacies of the swing. There are only four steps to take; master them and you will be a golfer.

THE SWING

Just four things you have to do to hit the ball well

Grip

First the dull bit. The first time anyone picks up a golf club he instinctively grasps it in the way which feels natural and strong. Since we are all different this instinctive approach results in some curious variations on the conventional golf grip. Many young right-handed children grasp the club with the left hand below the right. The commonest fault is to hold the club as if it were a two-handed sword and the embryonic golfer now looks like a Crusader preparing to slice off a Saracen's head. Unless expert advice is applied at that moment then the novice golfer is doomed. If he starts to play with a bad grip he will become a bad golfer and that is all there is to it.

Throughout the entire twentieth century, professional golfers have been preaching the message that good golf starts with a good grip and for the most part that excellent advice has been ignored. Human nature being what it is, the learner produces a persuasive counter-argument. 'What do these experts know about me? I am the only person who knows how I feel and I am certain, absolutely *positive,* that I can hit the ball better if I hold the club my way. What's more, I am equally sure that if I did hold the club with that uncomfortable Vardon grip I would not be able to bust a grape.' Sorry, but the voice which is whispering this advice about trusting to natural instincts is talking rubbish. A bad grip will breed a bad swing and together they will produce bad golf. Worse, there is nothing more difficult in golf than changing from a bad grip to a good one. Once that bad grip has become an engrained habit it takes months and months of hard work and frustration to change it. Even so, it is worth the agony. Unless a golfer plays to a low handicap the odds are a pound to a penny that his grip needs adjustment. Get the grip right and a good many faults in the swing will automatically disappear.

At this point we might as well clear up some misconceptions about good and bad grips. How can the way you hold a golf club be good or bad? Well, we are not talking about correct golfing behaviour, in the sense that table manners require us to hold a knife and fork in a certain way. In the context of golf, a good grip means an effective grip, an efficient grip for the specialized task of swinging a golf club.

It may help to understand something about the mechanics of the golf swing. When you swish a 13-oz club it seems that you are whipping the club-head through with a positive flick of the wrists, like cracking a whip. That is how it feels, but actually your feelings play you false. Impulses travel along the nervous system at the speed of sound but, fast as this may be, the speed of the downswing is so fast that there is a distinct delay in those messages reaching the brain. What you feel at any moment during the downswing actually occurred a split second earlier. The sensation you experience just before impact relates to what was happening when your hands were about hip high on the downswing. That is actually where your whiplash with the wrists occurs. By the time the club-head comes into contact with the ball the wrists have done their

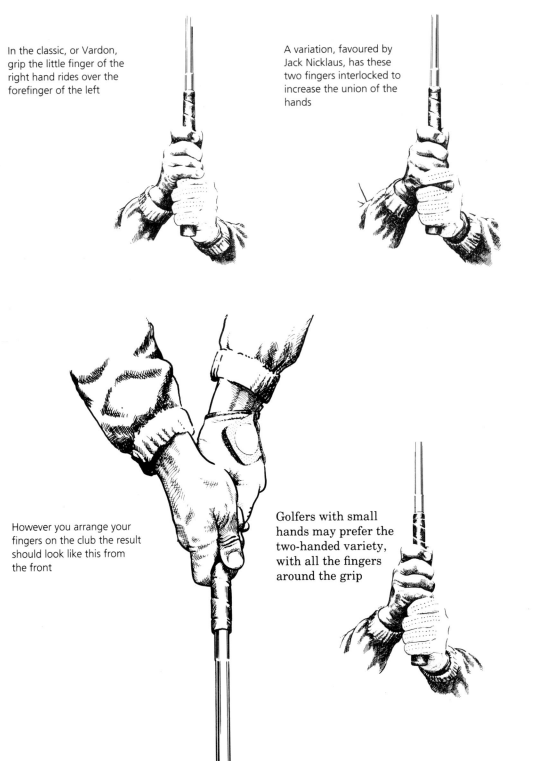

In the classic, or Vardon, grip the little finger of the right hand rides over the forefinger of the left

A variation, favoured by Jack Nicklaus, has these two fingers interlocked to increase the union of the hands

However you arrange your fingers on the club the result should look like this from the front

Golfers with small hands may prefer the two-handed variety, with all the fingers around the grip

work and are acting solely as free-swinging hinges. Immense forces build up during the business part of the swing. The weight of the club in your hands increases from a few ounces to a pull down the shaft of 110 lb. The club-head, travelling at about 100 miles an hour, meets the ball with an impact value of a ton-and-a-quarter. Knowing these facts will not help you play better but they may make you understand that an effective grip is necessary.

Imagine you had a door with one hinge out of alignment and that you then slammed the door. Screws would pop and splinters of wood would fly – and that is pretty much what happens when you swing a golf club with a bad grip. Plus, of course, the sad result that your ball flies into the rough – or worse. A bad grip will also refer strains to other parts of the body and the golfer's disease, back-ache, can often be cured by curing the grip. No matter whether you are just taking up the game or whether you have been playing for twenty years, you can make no more valuable investment in your future pleasure and satisfaction than by acquiring a good grip. You can acquire a good grip by studying diagrams and some people may do better with one of the recognized variations such as the interlocking style, as favoured by Jack Nicklaus, or the two-handed grip which Dai Rees employed so effectively over his long career. The vital consideration is that the wrists should work together, like door hinges in meticulous alignment.

At first a good grip feels weak and unnatural and rather clumsy. Persevere with it. Your muscles will adjust and in time the grip will feel strong and natural. Quite the easiest way of acquiring the priceless gift of a good grip is to take an old club, preferably a mid-iron, and have it fitted with a training grip. This is moulded so that the fingers fold into grooves and form a perfect Vardon grip. You cannot grip the club any other way.

For a month keep this practice club in your hands as much as possible. Hit practice shots with it. Do golf exercises (of which we will speak anon) with it. As you watch TV grip the club and inscribe love letters in the air with it, thereby strengthening your golf muscles and conditioning your hands to hold the club in a Vardon grip as second nature.

There are even a number of gardening jobs

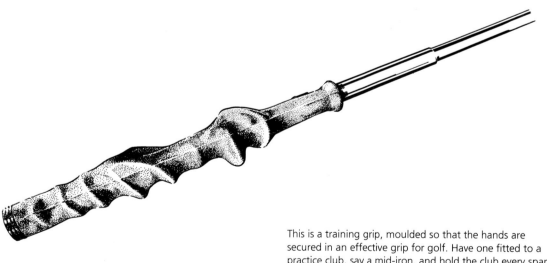

This is a training grip, moulded so that the hands are secured in an effective grip for golf. Have one fitted to a practice club, say a mid-iron, and hold the club every spare minute until you get accustomed to it and your grip feels strong and natural

which can be performed with the practice club, such as cutting down nettles, so you can feel virtuous while pursuing your selfish ends of training to become a hot shot golfer.

If you take nothing else from this book do, do, do, do acquire a good grip. It is by far the most important step to good golf.

Set-up

Why does it matter how you stand to hit a golf ball? Does a lumberjack have to be taught where to place his feet before he chops down a tree?

Yes, it does matter. The second of our four steps to an effective and repeating swing is a good set-up, or address position, and it is the easiest part of golf, absolute child's play. There is no opponent rushing at you to steal your ball; there is no time limit; there is no physical effort required; there is no complex mental problem to solve. All you have to do is to put yourself into the best position to hit the ball at your target and the most sensible idea is to establish a set routine which you follow for every shot. Even if you are on the practice ground with a pile of a hundred balls at your feet, it is wise to go through the entire sequence with each one of them. The idea should be to establish your set-up drill as a routine habit so that, as with gripping the club, you never have to think about it again and can concentrate all your mental energies on the shot you are about to play.

While watching TV inscribe passionate letters in the air to your lover with your practice club; hack down the weeds in the garden with it; beat the carpets and, if you must, the children with it. Nothing you do will pay richer dividends on the course than acquiring an effective grip

RIGHT: The pros call this the set-up and they all admire Severiano Ballesteros's set-up as the best in the business. Follow the five-stage drill and get into this position and you are half way to making a good shot

Step by Step in Setting Up for a Shot

1 Stand behind the ball and determine your precise target direction. Pick a mark just in front of the ball as an aiming point

2 Place the club-head behind the ball square to the line of the shot, using left hand only. Check club-face alignment against your aiming point

3 Settle your feet so you are standing at a comfortable distance from the ball, feet together and opposite the ball

4 Keeping the shoulders parallel to the target line, settle your right hand lightly on the club to complete your grip

The set-up sounds so straightforward (as indeed it is) that you might think you could just settle over the ball without the complication of a special drill. There are dangers in this lackadaisical approach. Experienced tournament professionals run into difficulties with their games from time to time and the reason is nearly always because they get out of position at the address. What happens is that imperceptibly they set themselves up with the ball fractionally away from its normal position, usually further forward. It may start with a deliberate change of address position, say for a shot from an uphill lie. Without their noticing it they set up with the ball further and further out of position.

They still hit good shots, of course, because they have the talent and experience to bring the club-head into the ball, but unconsciously they are making slight adjustments in their swings to compensate for the new ball position. Finally they reach the point where the distortion of the set-up

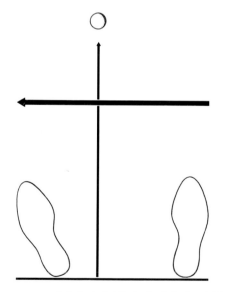

5 Now move your left foot slightly to the left, the right rather more so to the right. These distances will vary according to the club you are using. In this illustration, for a short chip shot, my stance will be quite narrow because I do not need a wide spread of the feet to maintain my balance

and the distortion of the swing combine to produce destructive shots, usually an attack of hooking, and they have to go back to the basics to find the source of the trouble. By now it is not just a case of establishing a proper address position again; all those compensating moves in the swing have to be eradicated by long hours on the practice ground. So it is much the best policy to establish a set drill and follow it every time, and then the problem will never arise. This is what you do:

1 Stand behind the ball so that your precise target, and the ball, and you are in line. This is the target line. Pick out some mark, a prominent blade of grass, worm cast or whatever, about a foot beyond the ball which is directly on the target line. That will be your point of reference when you come to swing the club through the ball. Now look up at your target again and visualize your shot. See the ball in your mind's eye soaring on a perfect trajectory, hanging in the air and than falling precisely on your chosen target. Even on drives, where your general aim is just to hit the ball as far up the fairway as possible, you should pick out an exact target, a precise area of fairway, which you judge to be comfortably within your range. (This way you will swing smoothly and by doing so you will very probably surpass your target by twenty yards or more.) Never just step up and belt the ball with all your might: you will be disappointed with the length of the shot and the direction as well, more than likely. All the time that you are setting up and making the shot keep in mind that vision of your ball flying straight at the target; that picture of your desired shot is all that your subconscious mind needs to programme your swing.

2 Holding the club in the left hand only, and with your proper left-hand grip, place the club-head half-an-inch behind the ball with the face exactly square to the target line. Use your point of reference and trust your instinct in squaring the club-face. Just as you can detect whether a picture on the wall is a degree or so skew-whiff, so you can trust yourself to square the club-face, provided that you look at the bottom edge of the club-face as

15

it rests on the turf. (With iron clubs the upper edge of the club-face may well appear to be angled to the right of your target.) In setting the club to the ball with the left hand like this you should see to it that the sole of the club is flat to the ground and the shaft is perpendicular. The club is now in the correct position at the ball and you have to keep it absolutely still as you position yourself on the club.

3 Place your feet together in such a position that your shoulders and hips are parallel to the target line, with ball and club bang in line with the centre of your body. How close should you be standing to the ball? Well, the rule is that you must feel natural and comfortable and for most people that means standing with the left arm hanging loosely and the butt of the left hand about four inches clear of the body.

4 Fold the fingers of the right hand on to the club, completing the grip. How tightly should you grasp the club at this stage? Apply about as much pressure as you would use in taking the hand of a small child to lead it across the road.

5 An average person using, say, a mid-iron should now move the left foot three inches to the left. Move the right foot about eight inches to the right. Dwarfs and giants will obviously have to vary these dimensions to suit their physiques, but the aim is to create a natural stance from which you feel confident of maintaining your balance. Clubs vary in length from about 42 inches to 36 inches and the width of your stance should be adjusted accordingly. With the woods and long irons the feet need to be wider apart to create a firm base for the wider swing. As you get down to the other end of the scale with the short irons the feet will be closer together. The important thing is to feel natural and comfortable; if you spread your feet too far apart you will inhibit the turning of the hips and shoulders. Although you vary the width of your stance the position of the ball should remain constant in relation to the left foot, about an inch inside the point opposite your left heel.

6 Flex the knees *slightly,* just enough to produce a feeling of preparedness for action. From a good golfing stance you should feel ready to skip a rope, or throw a punch, or dodge a punch, or leap in any direction. Forget anything you may have heard or read about having 62 per cent of the weight on the left foot, or favouring the weight on the balls of the feet. Just feel relaxed and ready for action, while standing tall and proud. Don't hang your head in shame; save that for when you miss a two-foot putt. No slovenly stooping, now. Nice straight back, but don't overdo it. The last thing we want in golf is muscular tension. Don't frown or clamp your teeth like a vice so that the veins on your neck stand out like hawsers. Golf is play, not war, and you are supposed to enjoy it. The shot you are about to hit is going to be pure bliss; anticipate that pleasure by releasing all tension from your body and your mind. Unwind. Think languid. You have your mental image of the ball tracing its path against the blue sky on its unerring progress to the target and now you are ready to savour the reality. And the way you will create that reality is by playing the shot as if you were miming a slow motion action-replay of a golf swing.

Swinging

With a good grip and a good set-up you are now more than halfway along the road to making a good shot. There are only two more things to do:

1 You must take the club-head back and raise it into a position from which you can make the most effective attack on the ball, and

2 You must perform this action at a speed which enables you to maintain absolute control over the club-head every inch of the way.

Sandy Lyle uses a short back-lift and generates his power with a strong component of hit. Experiment and discover which style is best suited to your physique and personality

The Feel of the Golf Swing

Imagine that you are swinging water in a bucket with a fixed handle. You will naturally accelerate smoothly as you take it back and you will naturally pause fractionally at the top to allow the water to change direction without spilling

Again, as you come down you will not heave violently at the start of the downswing, the ruination of many shots, but you will let the acceleration build up gradually. Your aim is maximum speed at the *bottom* of the arc, not before

As the bucket/club approaches the bottom of its arc you apply your surge of power, hurling the bucket/club through the impact zone along the line of the swing. The impetus of this action pulls you through to a stylish high finish

Some instructors seek to break down the swing into segments, exhorting their pupils to take the club-head back to position A and then move to position B, checking all the while that the weight is shifting to the inside of the right foot and that the right elbow is tucked tightly into the side of the body and that the left is ramrod straight. The poor novice, his head swimming with a hundred details, is now supposed to fuse this mass of instruction into one flowing movement. It is like asking him to memorize the cockpit drill for a jumbo jet and to check every point in the space of half-a-second. It cannot be done.

That is not to say that the instructions are incorrect. The left arm *is* kept straight during the golf swing. But this is one of the *effects* of making a good swing, not a *cause*. The aim must be to follow one simple instruction. Get that one thing right and all the hallmarks of a classical swing will follow naturally. Millions of words have been written about leg action, for instance. Ignore them. Your legs will behave exactly like Jack Nicklaus's without any conscious thought on your part if you obey your one all-important instruction.

That instruction is simple, but, since we are trying to combine two of golf's four essential elements into one image, embracing both what to do and the speed at which that action must be performed, we must approach this vital part of the golf swing in a leisurely, careful manner. After all, if you perform the right action and do it at the wrong rhythm you will be in trouble. Likewise, if you have perfect rhythm but perform the wrong action then you will not make a good shot. The two must go together and the best way to think of the golf swing is to recall the childhood game of swinging a bucket of water over your head without spilling a drop.

If you like, you can repeat the experiment just to revive your memories of how that game feels. Get a large bucket of water and grasp the handle with your golfing grip.

You are now going to swing it as high as you can without spilling any water, and as it descends you are going to accelerate it and throw the bucket over a low hedge. That is golf. In order to perform this exercise you naturally follow all the precepts of a good golf swing. You must start slowly and your body must turn and your arms must be kept straight.

You have to pause imperceptibly at the top of the swing so that the water, held in the inverted bucket by centrifugal force, makes the transition from upswing to downswing in its own good time. (The worst fault in golf is rushing this change of direction; that is what we call hitting from the top.)

Now, as the bucket descends, you feel naturally the right moment to accelerate its progress in order to throw it as far as you can over that hedge.

Apply that extra 'oomph' at the same point in the downswing when you are using a golf club and you will hit your maximum distance.

Rhythm

Of course, a club is much lighter and you will feel that you can apply much more force with it. You can certainly expend more energy, but it will not result in more distance. All that will happen is that you will lose control of the swing and the ball will almost certainly be mis-hit. Swinging the bucket will generate the highest club-head speed and that is what does the business in golf; sheer muscle power will not increase the clubhead speed.

That flowing, languid action of swinging the bucket, with the smoothly accelerating movements going up and coming down, is the *rhythm* of the swing. The tempo is the total time which elapses between taking the club back from the ball and returning it to impact. This can be fast or slow, provided the rhythm is maintained, and how fast you swing the club will depend on your build and personality. The general rule, no matter what your instinctive pace may be, is to swing more slowly than the speed you feel to be natural to you. Think of the bucket.

There is another very good reason to think of the bucket when you are practising golf on the driving range. Even though you may never have picked up a club you already know how to play golf. After all, you do not have to take lessons or read books in order to learn how to chop down a tree, or beat a carpet on the clothes-line, or sweep leaves on the garden path. You don't think about it, but just do it instinctively.

The subconscious part of your mind already has a pretty good idea of how to hit a golf ball if you can only bring yourself to let it get on with the job. However, golf is important. Pride is involved, and so are self-respect and lifelong conditioning to the idea that it is difficult. Therefore we make a conscious effort, telling ourselves to keep the left arm straight, watch that water hazard, keep your eye on the ball, shift the weight, and all the other rigmarole. The mind is like a gearbox with two gears

Every full stroke involves a combination of swing and hit. Ian Woosnam is one of the longest players in world golf and his action, long, languid and effortless, is almost pure swing

and we can only engage one gear at a time. The secret of golf, insofar as there is a secret, is to disengage the conscious gear and then let the unconscious gear operate the swing. The best way to do this is to give the conscious mind something to occupy its attention which will help the swing, rather than hinder it.

That is why 'tips' work. If the professional tells you to concentrate on digging the ball of the right foot into the ground as you come into the ball you may find that your golf improves immediately – but temporarily. Next day you will need a new gimmick. Provided that these tips have a golfing validity then they do help, not because of any secret ingredient they add to the swing but because they occupy the conscious mind and take it out of the act.

So when practising, think of the bucket and that thought will programme a good action and a good rhythm so that they become second nature. On the course, visualize the shot, with the ball flying towards your chosen target. In this way your conscious mind will be powerless to interfere with the mechanics of the swing.

Classical finish of a classical swing. The follow-through is the natural outcome of what has gone before and unless your finish is like Nick Faldo's there is something wrong. Check your basics

CHAPTER 2

DIAGNOSIS

The most maddening part of golf is the way form slips away overnight, for no apparent reason. You work hard and get to the happy stage, say, of driving the ball long and straight. You may feel that you have conquered this important component of your game. If so, you are in for a disappointment which will recur from time to time for the rest of your life. Nobody gets everything under complete control at the same time, which may be maddening for you, but just imagine what it does to a tournament professional whose living depends on his golfing form.

Anyway, glowing with satisfaction under the delusion that you have cracked the drive, the next time you go out to play you are shattered to discover that you have developed a slice, or a hook,

The Five Conditions for a Good Shot

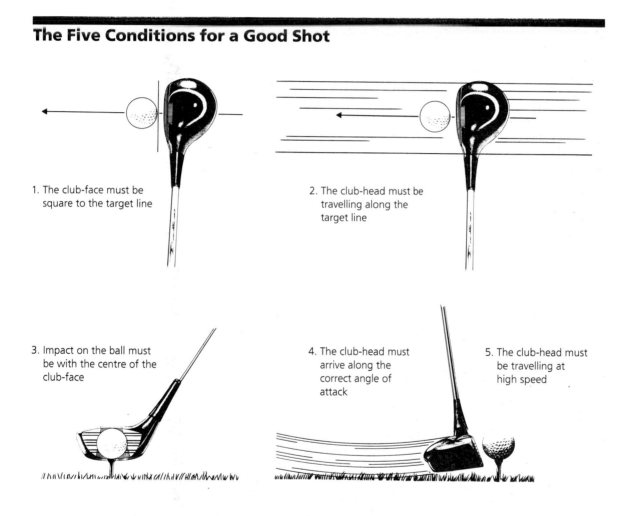

1. The club-face must be square to the target line

2. The club-head must be travelling along the target line

3. Impact on the ball must be with the centre of the club-face

4. The club-head must arrive along the correct angle of attack

5. The club-head must be travelling at high speed

LEFT: The American Peter Teravainen is the European Tour's longest driver and yet he does not appear to kill the ball. His secret, and it should be yours, is to concentrate on hitting the ball well, not hard

and, try as you might, you cannot put your finger on the cause. So far as you can detect you are not doing anything differently. However, the evidence of your ball curling away into the rough means that an error must have crept into your swing and it is important that you diagnose and correct the fault quickly. If you try to play your way out of the trouble you will almost certainly engrain the error and it will become that much harder to eradicate. You need a logical routine for pin-pointing faults, just as the motorist should set about tracing the cause of engine failure in a methodical manner.

The club-head governs the type of shot and it must comply with five requirements at impact if the shot is to be a good one.

If things go wrong

All bad shots are caused by an error in one of these five areas, or a combination of two or more errors. We can determine how the club-head is misbehaving by studying the flight of the ball.

If the shot is otherwise normal but the ball curls in flight to the right or left then we know that it is being influenced by sidespin. That is caused by a blow with a club-face which is angled, either open or closed. Again, this fault is normally associated with one or other error, in particular an incorrect angle of attack.

If the club-head approaches the ball in too steep a path of descent you will get less than the full value of the loft of the club and a 7-iron stroke will take off with the trajectory of a 3-iron stroke.

Conversely, too shallow an angle of attack, which means hitting the ball on the upswing, will either mean excessive elevation on the shot or, more likely, the club-head will skid on the turf behind the ball and catch it on its top half causing another of those frustrating scuffles along the ground.

Slices and Fades

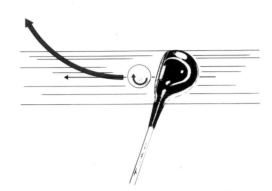

If the ball curls away to the right it means that the club-face was open at impact

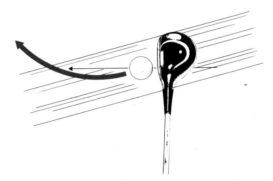

Regardless of the path of the club-head, an open face will send the ball curving to the right

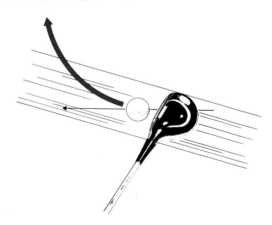

An in-to-out approach to the ball with an open face will send the ball out to the right and swerving further right

Pushes and Pulls

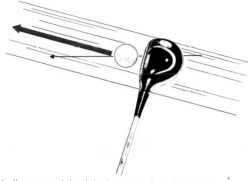

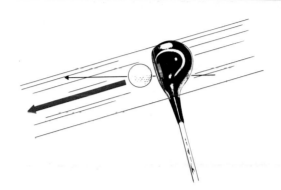

If the ball goes straight right it means that the club-head approached the ball from in-to-out with the club-face square

An out-to-in attack on the ball with a square club-face will send the ball on a straight line to the left

Hooks and Draws

If the ball curls in flight to the left it means that the club-face was shut, or hooded, at impact

Angle of Attack

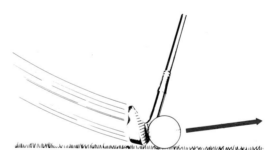

Too steep an angle of attack will reduce the loft of the club and give the ball an unnaturally low trajectory

Off-centre Problems

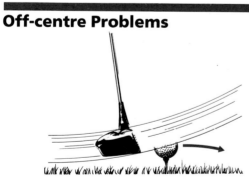

If the club-face meets the ball above the equator the impact will impart topspin and the ball will scuttle along the ground

Conversely if the club-head skids under the ball the shot will be skied, the ball popping up into the air with little forward momentum

Ronan Rafferty's largely self-taught action is proof of the old saying that your hands cannot be too strong for golf. Whichever style you adopt it will be much more effective if you build up hand strength

THROUGH THE BAG

Driving

The basic golf swing which you have now acquired is essentially a rotating action, with your body rotating on an imaginary axle in the region where our grandfathers used to wear their back collar studs. That is why the head is kept still during the swing; otherwise it would be like riding a bicycle with buckled wheels. Do not become neurotic about keeping your head still; it will remain motionless if you picture the swinging bucket without your paying any special attention to it. Obviously, any swaying will throw the axle out of kilter, but a rotation of the head on that axle is entirely permissible, indeed essential. This is particularly the case when using the driver, the only club with which you peg up the ball and with which you consciously try to hit the ball *up* as well as *forward*.

That picture explains one of the many paradoxes of golf. The club and arms are the spoke of a wheel which rotates on the axle and the swing is performed within an inclined plane, as if between two sheets of glass. However, the golfer's eyes are above that plane and from this viewpoint the player becomes the victim of an optical illusion. At impact, when the club-head is travelling directly along the target line it *looks* to the player as if it were travelling towards a point *to the right of the target*. The golfer must make a correction to take care of this illusion and a good way is to superimpose an imaginary clockface on the hitting area, with the ball in the centre and 12 o'clock straight

ahead. You should hurl your bucket and swing your club so that it enters the clockface at 4 o'clock, passes through the ball and leaves the clockface at 10 o'clock.

This is called 'hitting from inside to out', meaning that the club-head passes from inside the target line, through the ball and is thrown outside the target line. Having been initiated into the secret of that optical illusion you will realize that the expression 'in-to-out' is a load of baloney, although it certainly seems accurate as you swing.

Fairway Woods

With the exception of the straight-faced driver, you never try to help the ball go upwards. Of course you want it to rise, because golf is a game which is played through the air, but your club faces are angled to give loft, and this loft is all that is needed to send the ball soaring skywards. If you consciously try to scoop the ball into the air, all that will happen is this: you will fall back, and your club-head will catch the ball with its leading edge, sending it scuttling along the ground and very likely imparting a cut to its cover. That can be an expensive business, as well as a frustrating one.

Fairway woods are a joy. To clip a long shot off the turf into a distant green with a fairway wood is one of the supreme pleasures which the game has to offer. Many club golfers find them easier to handle than irons and pack their bags with six or seven of them, and in many cases a shot from long grass is easier played with a wooden club. Put your

The arms and the club form a unit like the spoke of a wheel which rotates on an axle located in the region of the back of the neck. It is this imaginary axle which must be kept absolutely still during the swing. The head may rotate on this axle during the swing but it must not be lifted prematurely in your anxiety to see the result of the shot. If you do that, you lift or tilt the axle which lifts the arm/club spoke and the shot is foozled

With every other club in the bag the loft of the club-face is sufficient to get the ball up into the air. The straight-faced driver however needs a little help and you should aim to contact the ball just as the club-head is starting its upwards sweep

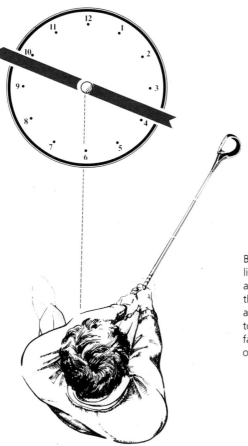

Because you are not looking at the ball straight down the line of the arm/club spoke, but have an oblique view from above the swing plane, you get a distorted perspective of the path of the club-head. What looks to you like a swing along the target line is actually a swing from slightly out-to-in. To correct for this optical illusion, superimpose a clock face on the ball and swing through from 4 o'clock to 10 o'clock

Bernhard Langer is known as the Iron Man, both for his steely character and his mastery of iron play. Conquer the long irons and you will be a complete golfer. Play practice rounds using only a 3-iron

Golf's most important paradox is that with the iron clubs you hit *down* in order to get the ball *up*. The idea is to contact the ball just before the club-head reaches the lowest part of its arc, so that the club-head hits the ball first and then goes downwards into the grass, scraping out a shallow divot of turf

trust in the loft of the club face to get the ball into the air, swing slowly and *sweep* the ball forwards, neither digging in nor scooping. The main consideration is to make a pure contact, with the leading edge of the club face getting right down level with the bottom of the ball. The broad soles of fairway woods help to make this precise contact as they skid on the surface rather than dig into the turf. Normally there is no divot from a clean fairway wood shot, just a scuffing of the grass.

Long Irons

Golf is riddled with mythology and one of the more persistent myths is that long irons are difficult clubs to use. There are two reasons why these dogs of long irons have been given a bad name. In the first place the relatively upright faces do not inspire the player with confidence in his ability to get the ball airborne. He thinks he has to help the process by scooping the ball into the air, with the unhappy results we have already seen. The second reason is that these are distance clubs and the player feels he must swing extra hard in order to get maximum benefit from them. The combination of these two misconceptions is more than enough to guarantee failure.

A normal swing, at normal tempo and rhythm, with a slightly downward angle of attack is all that is needed to play pure long-iron shots. The rule with all irons is to hit *down* in order to make the ball go *up*. You should never strain to get more distance out of a club than its natural worth. Tournament professionals who play with handicap golfers in pro-ams are appalled at the common macho attitude shown by their partners. The idea seems to be that there is more virtue in hitting a green with a 7-iron than with a 5-iron. It sounds so obvious as to be banal, but the virtue lies in *hitting the green*; what club you use is of no significance whatever. Boasting in the bar about 'getting up at the par-5 with a drive and an iron' may flatter your ego (and bore the hide off your friends) but such ambitions in golf are likely to prove extremely costly in lost bets. Underclubbing is the cardinal sin of club golf, all because of some spurious notion that a shot of 150 yards is supposed to be played with a 7-iron. That is rubbish. A shot of 150 yards may call for any club from the driver to the wedge. The correct club for any shot is the club which you feel confident will do the job, without straining.

An excellent exercise for building confidence in long-iron play, and dismissing those absurd notions about it being cissy to try a shot of 150 yards with anything more than a 7-iron, is to play a round of golf with only, say, a 3-iron. Beware of the temptation to slug with it off the tee. Just employ your normal swing with the tee shots and use touch and feel to manoeuvre your ball to the green. You will find bunkers and you can contrive shots to effect recoveries. Putt with the 3-iron. You will be astonished how well you can score with one club. Next time you have a spare hour or two, repeat the experiment with a 5-iron. Or a 7-iron. This is an excellent way to learn the variations on the standard shot and you will acquire confidence in those long irons, reaching for them like old and trusted friends when the need arises.

As explained in the section on the set-up, the stance will be slightly wider for the long irons and, since these clubs are longer, the arc of the swing will be wider. That means the club-head will approach the ball on a shallower angle of attack, with more of a sweeping action. Those technicalities need not cause you to make any conscious adjustments in the swing. You will automatically swing in a slightly more inclined plane to accommodate the longer shaft, and because of that shallower angle of attack you do not expect your divots to be so deep as you hit down and through the ball. The physical adjustments in the swing will take care of themselves if you can adjust your ideas about striving for maximum distance. The best way to play a 3-iron is to think about the way you play your favourite 7-iron as you make your swing.

Mid-Irons

The mid-iron range (5, 6, 7) represents the best of golf for many handicap players. The large faces and steeply angled loft fill the golfers with confidence to hit down and through the ball with complete assurance. For this reason it is not uncommon to come across a golfer of, say, 15 handicap who plays his mid-irons with the skill of a 6-handicapper. That is extraordinary, really, because if a golfer hits his 7-iron well there is no earthly reason why he should not be equally adept with every other club in the bag. Of course, as the numbers become higher, so the shafts become shorter and the clubs accordingly feel more manageable.

There are no fundamental changes in technique for mid-irons. Because the arm–club spoke is shorter, the wheel, or arc, of the swing becomes slightly smaller and thereby the club-head approaches the ball at a steeper angle. This means that divots are deeper, but this is the natural result of using the same swing, not because of any difference in method.

Short Irons

The short irons (8, 9, wedge) are the precision instruments of golf. At this end of the scale the need to balance the twin requirements of distance and accuracy changes emphasis. You still have to propel the ball forward, but instead of hitting it hard and straight you now concentrate totally on accuracy. You select the club which will give you the required distance but, knowing that this will happen without any special effort on your part, your sole concern should be to pick the landing area which you judge will leave your ball as close to the hole as possible and the feel of the shot is all-important. Power kills feel. The key to the short game is to employ the gift of touch. Whereas with the driver you were keyed up for a flowing swipe back over the bowler's head for a six, you should now be poised like a fly-fisherman about to drop a lure on to the nose of a trout.

In this phase of golf, your own instinct will be the best guide. Now you can relax your standard drill if you wish. Grip the club lightly in your fingers, imagine the ball floating up to the target and let your fingers dictate the routine. They may tell you to draw your left foot back slightly from the target line, so that you are standing slightly turned towards the target, or open. Don't worry about it. Don't even think about it. If it happens, well and good. After all, you do not think about what to do

With short irons the feel of the shot is rather like throwing a ball. You often see golfers actually mime the action of throwing a ball before they play these shots because it can be a valuable rehearsal in the tempo and effort needed for the stroke

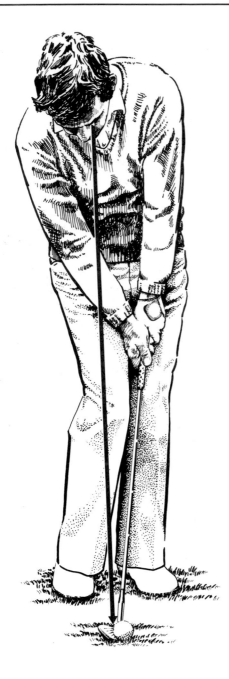

with your feet when you snatch up a cricket ball and send it smacking into the wicketkeeper's gloves with a crisp, underarm throw. That is what we are doing with golf's short game. Mentally lob the ball to the target and then repeat the action for real with a club in your hand.

The only danger to avoid with this throwing image is the tendency to scoop. Make sure you bring the club-head down and through the ball. There is not one shot in golf where the ball has to be scooped.

Short Game

Pitching and chipping are simply miniature versions of the short game. The same remarks apply, except that if you want to pitch the ball 30 yards you will not need to make a full swing. But although you shorten your backswing you keep the *same tempo and rhythm of a full swing.* Snatching is the ruination of delicate shots around the green. A pitch is a high lob played with a lofted club and a chip is a bounce-and-run shot with a straight-faced club. How do you decide which method to choose?

From a position close to the green your worst putt is likely to be as close as your best chip. So use the putter if the conditions are suitable.

If you have a shallow obstruction to clear, or if the intervening grass is thick, then take a mid-iron, say, a 7, and play the shot as if it were a long putt. You should aim to land the ball on the edge of the green and let it roll up to the hole. Get the ball on the ground and rolling as soon as possible. Your worst chip is likely to be as close as your best pitch.

If you have to carry an obstacle then, and only

The difference when you come to play the actual stroke is that, unlike the ball-throwing exercise, you must keep your eye rigorously on the ball rather than the target. Wait until you see your divot scrape before you look up

As a youngster Jose Maria Olazabal was a notably short driver. He amassed an unprecedented amateur record on the strength of his short game and putting. Practise your short game to save strokes

When to Chip and when to Pitch

Your worst putt will finish as close as your best chip, conditions permitting

Your worst chip will finish as close as your best pitch if you have to negotiate rough grass

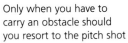

Only when you have to carry an obstacle should you resort to the pitch shot

then, play a pitch shot. Just because the pitch is third choice for short shots do not imagine that it is a difficult, last-resort shot. Far from it. The pitch is golf's equalizer, the shot with which a deft player can repair the damage of earlier errors. But it does require a special technique which must be learnt and practised. Use a wedge and lay the blade open, so that the natural loft is increased. Address the ball with an open stance (i.e. slightly turned towards your target) with the hands ahead of the ball and *most of your weight on the left foot*. For short pitch shots, and chips, the safest technique is to play this shot with the shoulders, keeping the arms pretty much out of the action. Turn away, as if starting a full backswing, but arrest this movement when you judge you have enough back-lift for the distance. Now turn back, allowing the club-head to follow through directly at your target. At the completion of the stroke you should be facing full on to your target. The usual exhortations apply: normal rhythm and tempo, a clean contact with a downward blow, full follow-through. A hurried pitch shot means almost certain failure. No stabbing or jabbing at the ball but a crisp, accelerating attack with the club-head.

Bunker Play

The first rule of sand recoveries is to eliminate fear. Do not fall into the habit of cursing and banging your club when you see your ball dive into a sand trap. Sand shots are just as much fun as any other golf stroke and they can be much, much more satisfying. If you approach them in this frame of mind, instead of bemoaning your bad luck, then you are halfway along the road to recovery.

Besides, the art of playing sand shots is not a rare gift bestowed by nature on one golfer in a million. Gary Player, who often plays into bunkers deliberately as the lesser of the two dangers, is not the favoured recipient of special powers; he is just a very good bunker player. You can be a very good bunker player too. Why not?

Let us deal with two common situations. (Practice and experience will teach the subtleties of special situations.) The most common bunker shot is the one from a bunker beside the green, where the player has to pop the ball up quickly so that it will land near the flagstick.

Abandon panic, anger and frustration and reach for your sand iron with a feeling of relish for the coming exhibition of recovery play with which you are about to astound your friends and opponents. Grip the club lightly and be sure not to allow it to touch the sand. That is considered to be 'testing the surface of the hazard' and incurs a penalty. Shuffle your feet well into the sand (which will tell you all you need to know about how soft the sand is) with an open stance. Favour the left foot to bear most of your weight. Address the ball with the face laid well open, almost horizontal, hands slightly ahead of the ball. In other words use your pitch shot technique.

Now imagine that the ball is sitting on a £5 note, with about two inches of the note projecting behind the ball. Your task is to scoot your clubhead through the sand so that it removes the note, along with the ball and the sand under it, without damaging the note. It will take quite a hard, descending blow and the rounded flange on the bottom of the club will stop the club-head burying into the sand. The manner in which the club-head strikes the sand is important. Imagine the clubhead to be a diver on the edge of the pool. He kicks off and cleaves the water with his extended fingers, the metaphorical equivalent of the leading edge of the club-head. What we want for bunker play is a belly flop, with the sole of the club making a hard pancake landing just behind the ball. The club-

(continued on p. 44)

OVERLEAF: Ross McFarlane gets up and down from greenside bunkers 85 times in 100 attempts. You know what to do. Just add a determination not to prod, lunge or jab but to make a full, wholehearted stroke

Golden rules for getting out of golden sand. Lay the face of your sand-wedge open and address the ball with an open stance, keeping as much weight as possible on the left foot. Make sure that you do not touch the sand with the club because that will incur a penalty for 'testing the surface'. Now imagine that your ball is sitting on a £5 note. Your objective should be to skim the club-head under the £5 note without touching it. Hit into the sand with a descending blow (the flange on the bottom of the club will prevent it from digging too deeply into the sand) and make it an attacking, accelerating stroke with a full, high follow-through. This is the standard explosion shot in which the club-head never actually touches the ball

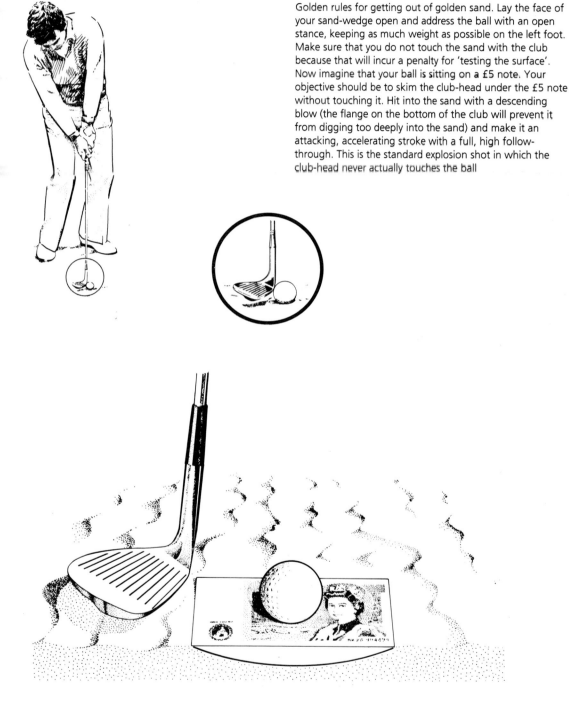

How to Vary the Distance of Sand Shots

The sand-wedge is the club for shots near the green and the technique for the stroke remains the same. To increase distance, progressively close the stance, bringing the position of the feet nearer to the target line, and make the club-head enter the sand at a point closer to the ball. . .

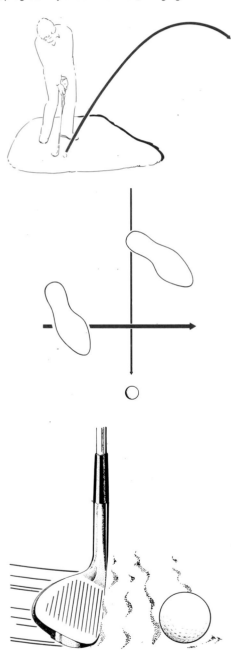

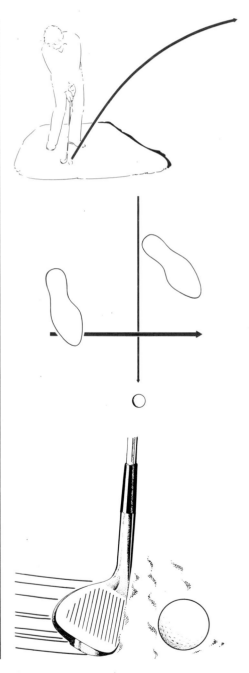

. . .And adjust the angle of the club-face, making it progressively less open. For full shots from fairway bunkers play a standard shot, as from the fairway, but aim to pick the ball cleanly off the top of the sand rather than hitting down and through the ball

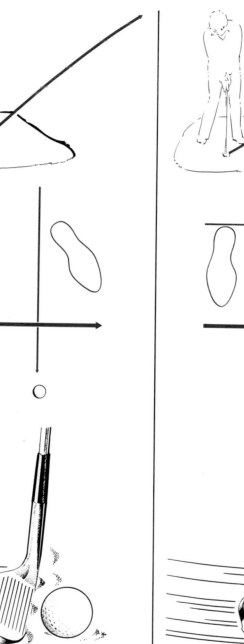

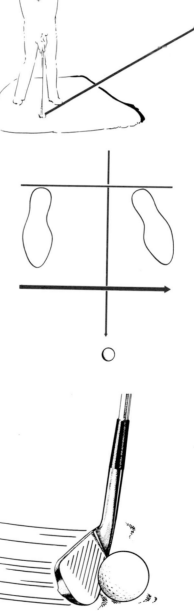

head has to really slap into the sand with plenty of forward momentum and the shot must be played with total conviction. Half an hour in a practice bunker will furnish you with the basic technique.

The key to this shot, as with every stroke in the book, is not to rush it or skimp it. Watch the great players. They take a full, slow backswing, keeping to their usual tempo and rhythm, pause, and then accelerate the club-head into the sand two inches behind the ball. It is not a stab; it is a proper golf shot with a lazy, high follow-through. It is not rushed and jerky, which is the way many handicap golfers come to grief; it is a slow but positive, attacking stroke. If the flag is a long way away, you adjust your imaginary £5 note and bring the club-head into the sand rather closer to the ball. Experience alone will teach you exactly how far behind the ball to enter the sand, according to the distance you want and the consistency of the sand.

The other common sand situation is a ball in a fairway bunker. On a modern course this is likely to be a shallow dish of a bunker and you will have every chance of playing just as good a shot as if your ball had been on the fairway. But if your club-head should dig into the sand before it makes contact with the ball then the shot will be killed. So here is one occasion where an exception must be made to the rule about hitting down and through the ball. It is more prudent in this case to use your fairway wood technique of sweeping the ball away, picking it cleanly off the top of the sand. Remember that in sand your footing is likely to be uncertain so it is vital to keep the backswing slow and controlled. Use plenty of the club for the job to avoid the temptation to overdo the power. If there is a pronounced lip on the bunker, or if you are in an old-fashioned pot bunker, then don't be greedy. Cut your losses and make sure of getting out, using the 'splash-shot' technique of greenside bunkers.

Putting

Every generalization about putting is either misleading or absurd, including this one. If we look at the outstanding exponents of this vital and tantalizing branch of golf, such as Bobby Locke, Jack Nicklaus, Bob Charles, Ben Crenshaw and Isao Aoki, it is impossible to pick out common characteristics which might provide the vital clues to their success. They all have individual techniques, so far as we can observe.

If you gathered together twenty of the world's leading professionals today, you might get general agreement on two essentials; that the head must be kept still, and that the left wrist should remain firm throughout the stroke. Yet both Locke and Aoki putt with flexible wrists, and nobody needs to be told to keep the head still while putting. You might as well instruct a seamstress to keep her head still while threading a needle. It happens naturally.

The difficulties which arise in putting do not often involve the simple physical act of making a pass with the putter. Putting is almost entirely a mental activity. The problems are in the mind, and that is where the solutions must be applied.

The kind of problems which may occur are: uncertainty over the precise direction and speed to strike the ball; tension of the kind that would arise if you took a simple action and tried to perform it on a tightrope; lack of confidence and failure of concentration. Any of those mental conditions, or combinations of them, will cause a putt to be missed. But if we can eliminate them and approach putting in a positive and healthy frame of mind, then the putts will drop no matter what technique we use.

Putt for dough! A regulation round of golf allows for 36 putts. Consider the advantage enjoyed by David Feherty who averages 28.5 putts a round and work on this vital game within a game

All putts are straight. At least it will help if you make them straight. From your calculations of the slope and swing, pick a target spot and then putt to that target as if you were on a dead flat surface

Uncertainty can be eliminated by going about putting in a businesslike manner, taking a good look at the line to the hole, noticing the texture of the grass to judge how fast the putt will be, noticing the direction and severity of any slopes and such pertinent factors as whether there is moisture on the surface. Try to avoid the conclusion that you are facing a difficult putt. Putting is supposed to be just as much of a pleasure as whacking a long drive, and the most effective response to a severe slope is to relish the extra challenge to your remarkable gifts.

Having noted all the factors which will affect the roll of your ball, you will automatically decide where to hit the ball, and how hard. Have trust in that decision. Make a note of a precise spot over which you want your ball to pass, and the speed

you want it to be travelling at that moment. Visualize your ball rolling along that path and toppling into the hole. Keep that image in your mind as you settle over the ball and line up the blade of your putter. Get yourself into a position which feels comfortable for making a stroke towards your target spot (which may not be the hole, of course, on a swinging putt).

Now ask yourself what the grass looks like directly beneath your ball and sweep the ball away so that you can satisfy your curiosity. This little mental trick has several beneficial results. Your nervous system has already been fully programmed as to the stroke you wish it to perform and by concentrating on this irrelevant question you allow it to produce the stroke without interference from your conscious mind. It also guarantees that

For level putts I like Ben Crenshaw's trick of imagining a welcoming red carpet the width of the hole. He then putts along the carpet – and who wouldn't envy his success rate on the greens?

you make firm contact with the ball and that you keep your head still until the ball is safely on its way.

Although putting is ninety-nine per cent mental, there are certain practical ways of helping your performance on the green. You have already established a set routine for approaching every shot and setting up to the ball. Since putting is so highly individual, you may adopt any routine which suits your personality, but it should incorporate the following features:

1 Survey your putt thoroughly, noticing the slopes and the way the grass lies (– the nap, or grain. Pronounced nap will have a marked effect on your putt). Pick out a target spot on the green and determine that this is where you are going to aim. *All putts are straight.* Never try to hook or slice a putt.

2 Find yourself a comfortable stance, one which allows you to keep your body *still* while allowing you perfect freedom to move the putter. Anything goes in putting stances provided it works for you.

3 Grip the putter lightly. This is the most delicate stroke of all and you need every bit of help you can get from the sensitivity of your hands. Do not crush that sensitivity by strangling the putter.

4 This is not an imperative, but generally speaking a firm left wrist, so that the putter is an extension of the left arm, is advisable for consistent putting. If you hole more than your share of putts with a loose-wristed action, then stay with your method. But if things should begin to go wrong, remember that tip about a stiff left wrist; it could save your sanity.

5 Above all, do everything you can to ease the mental pressure of putting. There is no doubt that the players who are most relaxed on the greens, both mentally and physically, hole the most putts. Of course, that is easier said than done; you cannot just tell tension to go away. But there are ways in which you can con your nervous system into tranquillity. Approach the task in a businesslike, positive manner, seriously but not too solemnly. Accept that you will not hole every putt and that the world will continue to rotate if you miss. Do not spend overlong agonizing over the problem; the longer you delay the stroke the more time you allow mental tension to build up and that will lead to physical tension. Enjoy it. Let Rudyard Kipling be your guide on the greens: If you can meet with Triumph and Disaster and treat those two imposters just the same – you'll be a putter, my son!

Uneven Lies

It might be stretching a point to say that more tosh has been written about the technique for playing from sloping lies than any other aspect of golf, for writing golf instruction is a massive tosh industry, but many recommendations for this aspect of golf are dangerous tosh. In particular we must vigorously reject the common suggestion that the golfer should emulate the stance of the leaning tower of Pisa in order to equalize the effect of sloping lies. That is just asking for trouble and quite possibly a sprained ankle.

The human body is a wonderful machine, a thousand times more effective than the most sophisticated computer, and you do not have to give it special instructions about how to stand upright on a slope. It does not take the body long to adjust to the rolling deck of a ship and the sailor is soon able to maintain his equilibrium while the slope beneath his feet changes pitch continually. If we can do that, then standing upright on a fixed slope is a piece of cake.

The first thing to do in assessing how to play from a slope is to be aware of how the uneven lie will affect the action of the club-head. The rule is that if you are playing uphill you must club up, that is, selecting a 4-iron for a shot which would call for a 5-iron on level ground. Playing downhill you club down.

In both cases be kind to yourself and be confident that you have plenty of club for the distance; it is more important than ever that you do not strain for distance on these sloping lie shots. Besides, because one leg must flex more than the other in stabilizing your stance, the arc of the swing will be fractionally shorter than usual. A clean, precise contact with the ball is the first priority.

Before taking your stance you must establish by how much to adjust to the position of the ball. On downhill shots the lowest point of your arc, the hitting zone, will be nearer the right foot than usual, and *vice versa* for uphill shots. You can determine by how much to adjust to the ball position by taking a practice swing and noting where the club-head grazes the turf. That should be the ball position. Follow your normal set-up drill and stand as comfortably as the slope will allow. Now play your normal shot.

For sidehill lies you follow the same routine. If the ball is below your feet you will obviously have

Uphill: ball forward slightly at the address

Downhill: ball played from further back

Ball above the feet: stand further back to accommodate a flatter swing

Ball below the feet: stand closer because your swing will be more upright

to stand rather closer to it than usual in order to reach it comfortably. That will give you a rather more upright swing plane and a shallower arc, so take one more club than normal. Also, because of the ball's unusual position, the tendency will be to fail to get right down and through the ball. The chances are that unless you are careful the shot will be topped or, if the error is not so severe, the shot will slice because of failing to stay right down and through with the club-head.

There is no necessity to become neurotic about these dangers. It is enough to remind yourself of the possibilities and to be aware of the special need to stay right down on the shot; it is a good idea to watch for your divot scrape before looking up. Just ask yourself what the turf under your ball will look like after the ball has gone, and you will ensure that your head does not come up prematurely.

Take your practice swing to find out just how closely you must stand to the ball to make a sweet, certain contact and away you go.

When the ball is above your feet the reverse applies. The ball will be further from your body, your swing plane flatter, your arc longer. The tendency will be to dig into the turf, exaggerating a desirable feature into a fault, and the combination of all these circumstances will produce a hook unless you take remedial action. All you have to do about it is to give yourself a gentle reminder of the possibility of a hook and then let nature take its course. As usual, your practice swing will determine how you should position yourself in relation to the ball.

Above all, when playing from slopes of any kind, you should avoid falling into the trap of regarding these shots as being from 'bad' or 'difficult' lies. They are not bad, they are different. All they need is a slightly different stroke. Apply the differences in a positive frame of mind and the ball will behave just as obediently to your wishes as if it were struck from a level lie.

Indeed, you should aim to adopt this neutral philosophy to your entire game. Keep your emo-

tions on an even keel. Suppress your elation when you hit an approach close to the flag and resist disappointment when your ball goes into a bunker. These events are not matters for rejoicing or despair; they are simply the outcome of the laws of nature and you will improve more quickly if you accept them as such.

By the same token you should avoid thinking in terms of 'good' and 'bad' luck. There is no such thing as lucky bounce; a ball bounces in a certain direction because it lands on a piece of ground set at a certain angle. There is no supernatural force which can alter that bounce by so much as a millimetre. If your ball goes into a bunker there is only one reason – because you hit it there. Accept that fact dispassionately like a neutral observer plotting the fall of shell fire, and the next time you play that stroke the chances are that the ball will not go into the bunker.

A child does not curse his luck when he topples over while taking his first tentative steps; he does not determine that next time he will put a bit more weight on the right foot and point his left foot fractionally more outwards. The child just gets up and tries again; his body has absorbed the lesson of that last experience and automatically makes the necessary adjustment. This time he manages two more steps before he goes down. He does not curse the uneven carpet, or claim that he was the innocent victim of malicious fate. He gets up and his nervous system makes a further adjustment in the control system. The only conscious input the child makes to the programming of his control system for walking is a determination that he is going to get the hang of walking.

That essentially is the message of this book. The element of actual teaching has been kept to the minimum, amounting to no more in the walking metaphor than making sure there is a guard over the fireplace and that the cat is not asleep on the carpet in the path of the child.

If you can approach golf with the innocence of a child, absorbing experiences with an open mind, then the game will be learnt. Learning is a much surer process than being taught, and progress much quicker. There are wealthy golfers who have had regular weekly lessons for years and years, from a hundred different teachers, and they do not improve by a stroke. They become so confused that their learning powers atrophy. This is not to say that a good instructor cannot help you. If possible it is advisable to have a good professional monitor your progress, checking that you have acquired those four basics and that you are not falling into bad habits.

Golf is almost totally a mental game. If you apply your conscious mind to the tactics of making the game as simple as you can and let your unconscious mind get on with its proper function of learning the technique of swinging a club, then you will become a real golfer. But if you reverse that process, concentrating your conscious mind on swing technicalities and allowing your unconscious mind to dictate your tactics, then you will surely be a hacker for the rest of your life.

In no phase of golf is this lesson more important than in acquiring confidence with uneven lies. If possible, find a mound in a suitable practice area and experiment with different lies. Follow the suggestions given above and hit shots, noting the flight of the ball but without trying to analyse what you are doing wrong. Just tell yourself 'that one went left' and try again. The shots will straighten themselves out if you allow your subconscious to learn its lesson. Hit a few good ones to reinforce the message and move to a new challenge as you work your way around the mound.

THE CURE

By studying the flight of wayward shots we now have a clear idea of the nature of the disease and we are ready to start prescribing remedies for a cure. There are only four components to check – grip, set-up, the position at the top of the back-swing and the rhythm – and it is a sensible policy to give your swing a regular inspection, like having your car serviced.

The grip is a prime source of hooks and slices and once a grip fault develops it is not long before the golfer begins to make compensations and the swing is adversely affected. Two possible sources of error in the grip are the actual formation of the hands on the club and the tension of the grip.

All golfers of every level undergo changes in sensitivity of their hands. One day your hands feel lean and strong and dextrous, and another day they feel puffy and clumsy even though they look exactly the same. On those days when nature seems to have equipped you with a bunch of insensitive sausages instead of fingers you may well react by unconsciously gripping the club too tightly and that in turn will tighten the arm and back muscles sufficiently to inhibit a free swing.

A good way to check your grip is to grasp the club in the usual way, at the usual gentle tension, and then to lift your arms to shoulder level, so that the club is held straight out in front of your eyes. Now tighten your grip on the club as hard as you can, as if trying to throttle it. Keep your eye on the club-face. If it rotates, either opening or closing as you tighten your grip, then you have discovered your fault. At impact there will be considerable forces to be resisted; the club-head will increase in effective weight under centrifugal force until it is exerting a pull down the shaft equivalent to the weight of a sack of potatoes, and your grip must be equal to the task of hanging on to the club without twisting the club-face.

This tightening process will happen quite naturally, without your doing anything about it, and you should not consciously tighten your grip during the swing. But, knowing that it is going to happen, you will appreciate how vital it is that you grip the club in such a way that, when the tightening process *occurs*, you do not inadvertently turn the club-face open or closed.

Once you are reassured that your grip is not causing your problem, the next component to check is the *set-up*. If you are meticulously following your set-up routine you might imagine that nothing could go wrong in that department, but it is surprising how often bad habits creep in without the player noticing. Golfers who have to drive a long way to the course may develop a stiffness in the back without realizing it and unconsciously take up an open stance in order to take some strain off their spines. The difference may be fractional and the consequences equally fractional: a shorter backswing and a slight variation in the arc of the swing. But by the time these variations are magnified in the club-head, whipping into the ball at a hundred miles an hour slightly off line, they are enough to produce disastrous shots. So go back to basics and make sure that your set-up is correct. Pushes and pulls derive from a bad set-up and always remember that an otherwise perfect set-up is a bad one if the ball is out of position.

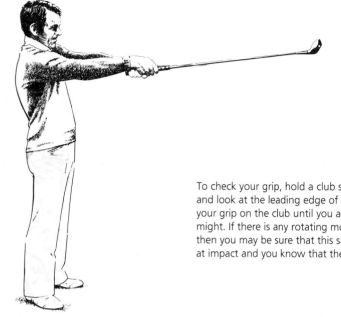

To check your grip, hold a club straight out at arm's length and look at the leading edge of the club-face. Now tighten your grip on the club until you are squeezing with all your might. If there is any rotating movement of the club-head then you may be sure that this same movement is occurring at impact and you know that the fault lies in your grip

Anxiety

The prime cause of bad shots is anxiety. Once a golfer becomes anxious not to drive into the woods, or not to lose a hole, or to extricate his ball from a difficult lie, or not to ruin his score, or simply not to make a fool of himself, then he becomes a prime candidate for a bad shot. Mental tension will express itself in the last of our vital components of golf, in *turning into a position from which to attack the ball* and even more so in *maintaining a tempo and rhythm which enables him to keep control of the club-head throughout the swing*.

This is what loses championships and what separates the great players from the also-rans. It manifests itself in a shortening and speeding up of the backswing. Often the player fails to turn, simply lifting the club with his hands, and this causes a loss of club-head speed and a narrowed arc, with an increased angle of attack on the ball. Anxiety is also a prime cause of increasing the tension of the grip.

Since the cause is in the mind, it is here that the cure must be applied. Telling yourself to relax is not the answer; that is like telling a fire to go out. After all, anxiety is a perfectly natural response to a difficult or frightening task. Experience is the best treatment. It is axiomatic in golf that the first time a player faces an anxious problem, whether it is pitching over a bunker or facing a three-footer for the Open Championship, he fails. The second time he is subject to the same stress situation he may well succeed. If so, his anxiety will subside and he will face that problem with equanimity the next time he encounters it. But that is not to say that he will never again be subject to anxiety; it simply means that he has pushed back his anxiety threshold.

53

If there is an inconvenient bunker at exactly the distance which you normally drive, then you can remove the bunker from the course, and from your nerves, by selecting a club which you know will not send the ball that far. This is one of Lee Trevino's favourite gambits and this kind of game management is one reason he is so difficult to beat. I should know!

There is nothing like water for dissolving a golfer's confidence, but you can outwit it. As you survey the aquatic horrors ahead, superimpose a scene which holds no terrors for you. In this example, the imaginary scene is a practice ground. You have no problems with hitting a shot of 150 yards on the practice ground and, by the use of a little imagination, that is now all you have to do

Jack Nicklaus still feels anxiety on the golf course, for all his huge experience of winning the world's greatest championships, because he is still meeting new situations, facing novel challenges. He is a good example for all golfers to copy because he turns his emotional tension to his own advantage. He relishes a feeling of anxiety because he appreciates that fear heightens the senses and increases the physical capacity of the body. Good, he tells himself when his pulse begins to race, I am now much better equipped to pull off this difficult shot, or to play out this tight finish. He reinforces this advantage by recognizing that if *he* is experiencing anxiety then his less experienced rivals must be in the grips of the same, or worse, fears and they have fewer resources to combat them. So Nicklaus is elevated by anxiety while the others are downcast by it; that is the true power of positive thinking.

We can all benefit by taking a leaf out of the Nicklaus book, from the novice to the experienced professional, and the best way is to start by drawing the sting from the source of anxiety. When your inner voice starts your nerves jangling by drawing attention to a looming fairway bunker sited just at the spot where your drive is likely to finish, you can defuse your fears by following Lee Trevino's policy. He assesses which club he can use so that even if he hits his Sunday-best shot flush off the centre of the club-face the ball will roll to a halt short of the hazard. He has thus effectively eliminated the bunker and plays his shot in perfect peace of mind.

Let us try some other tranquillizing tricks. Water is a powerful source of anxiety and when you have to play a shot over an expanse of water there is no point in using Trevino's trick of laying up short. That would be simply postponing the ordeal and wasting a stroke. Work out the distance calmly and pick a target landing area on the far side of the water. Let us say that it is 165 yards away. Now, you know very well that you are perfectly capable of hitting a ball 165 yards. You have played this shot hundreds of times. The only thing which com-

plicates this particular shot is that intimidating water. At such times it helps enormously to recall a situation which calls for an *easy* shot of 165 yards. Well, it is easy enough on the practice ground, isn't it? Superimpose an image of the practice ground on the scene. There is the 150-yard marker straight ahead. Now the prospect is not daunting at all. Just play your usual shot over that marker.

This trick is a variation on the tunnel vision which all good players employ. Some golfers actually survey a shot by placing their hands alongside their heads, like blinkers, so that all they can see is the green, with bunkers, trees, lakes, eclipsed by their hands. It is one way of thinking positively about the target and not negatively about the potential dangers.

Another source of anxiety is the bunker shot, especially for golfers who have not thoroughly mastered the technique of sand play. Obviously there is no mental trick you can employ to eliminate a hazard if your ball is actually in the middle of it. It is here, in bunkers around the green, that unskilled golfers betray their anxiety by shortening and speeding their backswings, turning them into hacking convulsions. Here, above all, success depends upon maintaining a full backswing and a measured tempo and rhythm.

Often a difficult (and fearsome) bunker shot can be turned into an easy (and carefree) shot just by appraising it in a positive frame of mine. Say, there are only three yards of green between the lip of the bunker and the flag, offering your fevered imagination only the tiniest of targets for you to pop your ball on to the edge of the green so that it will run and stop short of the hole. Wait a minute and take another good look. There is no reason why you should be aiming to stop the ball this side of the hole. It is more than likely that you will have an easier putt coming back from the other side of the hole. In that case you double the size of your target area and suddenly the shot will become that much easier. You have a margin for error and play with an assurance that had seemed impossible a few moments earlier. It is surprising how often in

Have you ever wondered why professional golfers sometimes hold their hands alongside their heads like blinkers? We do that to block out the sight, and therefore the destructive thoughts, of hazards and other trouble. This picture frame achieves the same purpose. There is no trouble in the frame and it encloses a generous target area. The shot is a piece of cake

57

It would need an incredibly delicate shot to splash the ball out of the bunker and stop it short of the flag. Difficulty means tension. However the situation is transformed if you think in terms of a recovery shot past the flag. That is a doddle. The only difference is that your putt will be from a different direction. But by choosing the easy option you will play the stroke with confidence and probably get it closer

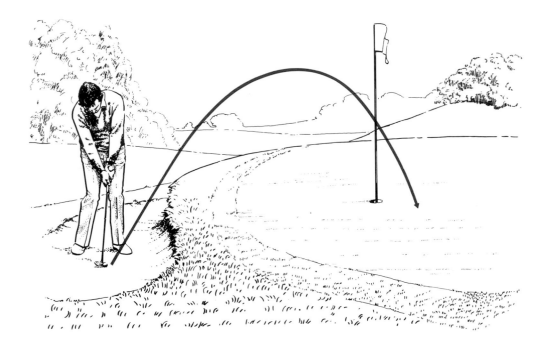

these cases where you enjoy a little mental triumph, simplifying a shot by using your wits, that you put the ball close to the hole.

Once you have mastered the basic golf swing and are hitting solid shots, you will be anxious to introduce those refinements which will enable you to curve your shots right and left, in controlled fades and draws, and so cut some corners on the course. The facility to move the ball sideways through the air makes an immense contribution to your capacity for positive thinking because it doubles the width of every fairway. When you see a golfer reach for an iron on the tee of a tight hole you may be sure that he is responding negatively and putting himself at risk of the most embarrassing and frustrating experience the game has to

offer, deliberately playing safe and hitting the ball into the woods. But the golfer who is confident of his ability to hit a controlled fade or draw can turn a 50-yard fairway into 100 yards by aiming down one side and allowing the ball to ease back into the middle of the fairway.

That raises the question of how to impart that priceless sidespin. The best answer was provided by Sam Snead. 'How do you deliberately slice a ball?' he was asked. Snead pondered the question for a moment and answered: 'I think slice.'

But what do you *do*, you are probably asking. After all, you must do something different in the swing to impart a deliberate fade. Well, many instruction books do go into detail on adjusting the stance and even the grip for fades and draws.

Snead's way is much better. Make no changes at all in the preparation or the actual swing. Just visualize the ball curling gently into the air and then play your normal shot. Provided that you are quite clear in your mind how you want the ball to move your hands will make the necessary adjustments without any conscious help from you. Try it. Go to the practice ground and hit alternate fades and draws by what you may imagine to be the power of suggestion alone. By all means experiment. Hitting bad shots will programme your unconscious mind with valuable information about the swing, but do not fall into the pernicious habit of concentrating on fragmented details of technique.

For fades you may find it helpful to draw the left foot backwards an inch or so from its usual address position and to play the ball half-an-inch to the right of its normal position. By the same token, a slight withdrawal of the right foot at the address and a positioning of the ball fractionally to the left of its regular site may assist with the fade. Do not overdo these adjustments and, for preference, learn to hit your fades and draws from your normal set-up. That is the simple way and that is the way which your subconscious mind will master most readily. Visualize those valuable fades and draws and just let them happen. Think slice.

Topped Shots

These days the covers of golf balls are virtually indestructible, unless you specify the traditional synthetic rubber covers, and yet balls which you find on golf courses, abandoned by their frustrated owners after the legal five-minute search, often bear the unmistakable marks of topped shots. The balls may no longer gape with open grins but the smiles are discernible and they bear witness to one of the least amusing errors in the game.

Topping is a misery because the ball scuttles along the ground for pathetic distances and the player feels that he is not engaged in golf at all. Hitting towering shots which soar away in the wrong direction is bearable, because the player rightly feels that he needs only a minor adjustment in the steering system and he will be a fine golfer. But topping induces despair. A succession of topped shots threatens the golfer's self-respect and brands him as a rabbit, or duffer. As a result he makes Herculean efforts to get the ball airborne by scooping, and the only result is that the topping becomes worse.

The answer is to go back to those four basics – the grip, the set-up, the position of the top of the back swing and rhythm. The mental image of that swinging bucket of water should bring the clubhead into the ball on a descending path, but if it fails then stronger remedial measures are clearly necessary. Imagine that there is a small croquet hoop about a yard in front of the ball on the target line. Instead of trying to get the ball up into the air, your aim should be to keep it low, hitting it through that hoop. Golf is a game of paradoxes and this is the most striking example: in order to get the ball *up* you have to hit it *down*.

Slicing

Here is another paradox. Unintentional slicing is a common fault, with the ball curling away in a sickening curve into the rough on the right, or into the woods, or out of bounds. The natural tendency is to counter the slice by aiming further left, but all that happens is that the slice gets worse and the ball still flies into that right-hand rough.

The cure is to aim deliberately towards that hateful rough on the right of the fairway. Set up to the ball with everything pointing down the right side, feet, shoulders and club-face. Now make sure that you make a good *turn* as you swing that bucket of water to shoulder height, bringing the clubhead *inside* the line as you take it away from the ball. So far, you may feel, you have made a thorough preparation to miss the fairway on the right once more. But no. Trust your swing and the laws of dynamics. Complete the backswing with

If topping is your problem or, indeed, if you have trouble getting the ball airborne, then there is a simple remedy at hand. Just imagine that there is a croquet hoop about four feet in front of you, directly on your line. Now try to hit the ball through the hoop. It will soar over the top every time

Some golfers can get away with a slight sway into the ball but any swaying as you take the club back is the ruination of a shot. The habit is easily enough cured with a session on the practice ground by tucking a ball under the outside of the right shoe. This not only stops any tendency to sway but it also induces the correct platform for the swing, like a boxer getting poised to throw a punch

your usual measured rhythm, allow the club-head to reverse direction in its own good time and then attack the ball along that 'in-to-out' line, from 4 o'clock to 10 o'clock. As we have already explained, that in-to-out line is an optical illusion and your club-head will actually be travelling along the target line, producing a straight shot.

Of course, from your closed set-up position the straight shot will go down the right side of the fairway. To bring it back into the centre of the fairway, and incidentally to get a few yards extra on your drive, you have to master the art of what is called 'releasing' the club. We did not mention the release in the instructions for the basic swing because with a light grip on the club and a smoothly accelerating downswing it is something which happens naturally. However, a golfer with a swing problem is almost certainly a tense golfer and that means he will be hanging on to the club for dear life and inhibiting a free release.

Some instructors describe the release by recalling the feeling of whipping a top, or cracking a whip. Some speak of 'throwing the club-head at the ball'. These images are all very well, and many golfers find them useful, but there is a danger that they could result in a flicky action, which is not quite what is wanted.

For purposes of acquiring the feel of a good release, assume that the head of your club has been attached to the end of the shaft with glue which has not quite set. You want to get the club-head off. It is too firmly attached to pull it off, or waggle if off. So you swing the club and as it approaches the ball you put a surge of extra 'oomph' into your action. It is the same technique that you use to flip off a sticky sweet stuck to your finger. As a matter of fact, if your club-head did actually come unstuck and detach from the shaft as you were releasing the head at the ball, the shot would be exactly the same as if you were using a normal club.

Another way to acquire the feeling of release is to tie a weight on a piece of cord about the same length as a club and whirl it around in a golfing arc. As the cord cuts through the air it will create the familiar whirring noise and the object is to make the cord really sing *whizz!*, as the weight reaches the lowest point of its arc. You slicers should practise this exercise, swinging the weight slowly, just fast enough to keep it at full extension on the end of the cord and then whizzing it at maximum speed through the hitting area.

Repeat that action with a club, whizzing the club-head through the ball and allowing your forearms to follow their natural tendency to roll, right over left, through the impact zone. That action, allied to an in-to-out attack on the ball, will impart a hint of anti-clockwise spin, producing a beautiful controlled draw which will direct the ball into the middle of the fairway.

The dreaded slice, the bane of club golfers, can be eliminated with a little application. Often it is caused by excessive body power and not enough action of the hands and arms. More zip with the hands is needed in the impact zone. To acquire this hand speed, take a piece of cord about the length of a golf club and attach a weight to it. Swing it either like a golf shot or in a continuous rotating movement like a helicopter. Listen to the noise made by the cord as it cuts through the air. The effect you want is a rising note, with a loud *whoosh!* as the weight passes the ball position

Repeat that exercise using a golf club and aim down the *right* hand side of the fairway – the very area of maximum danger for a slicer. The ball will start off in that direction but if you reproduce that *whoosh!* through the hitting zone, releasing the club-head freely as you did with the weighted cord, then the ball will curve gently from right to left in a beautiful draw and finish in the middle of the fairway

5

IN THE MIND

The three real secrets of golf – coolness, confidence and concentration

Coolness

Olympic sprinters have to push themselves to the very limit of their capacity, but for most of us the secret of a happy and tranquil life is to make an honest assessment of our capabilities and then throttle down a notch or two. In this way we can operate comfortably and confidently without strain or the risk of ulcers. Work becomes a breeze when we perform well within the limits of our skills and talents. This suggestion may sound like heresy to people who have been indoctrinated almost from birth in the sporting philosophy of giving 110 per cent effort in pursuit of success.

Sports coaches study psychological techniques in order to 'psych up' athletes to a point where a footballer is ready to die for the team, or a runner to summon unprecedented reserves of energy. The body cannot distinguish between this highly charged nervous state and fear, and the player who is emotionally pumped up triggers off a natural response which is designed for the preservation of the human race, called the 'fight or flight' syndrome. This is what spurs a timid man when cornered to lash out at his pursuers, what enables a frantic father to perform prodigious acts of strength such as lifting the front of his car off a trapped child, or what gives a hunted man running for his life a turn of speed of which he would not normally be capable.

Biologically these unsuspected reserves of strength are brought into action by the body switching off those functions which are not strictly

necessary for the moment of crisis. The digestive system slows down to the level where the psyched-up athlete may feel sick or even vomit. The nerves on the outer layer of the body switch off, which is why the hands feel cold and clammy and why a man fighting for his life does not feel pain from the blows being rained upon him. The trachea contracts during this process of concentrating all the body's energies into the essential survival areas, causing the familiar choking sensation and often affecting the vocal chords. Extra adrenalin is released into the system and the brain closes down the functions of reason and logic in order to boost the senses of hearing and vision to cope with the emergency. A person in this hyper-emotional condition is thus superbly equipped to battle his way through a maul of players and force his way over the try line. But his capacity to perform delicate or complicated actions is vastly impaired and his powers of reasoning are greatly reduced. In short, this is no way to play golf.

The golfer needs to psych himself *down* and one of the complications in competitive golf is that when the situation raises a player's emotional level, as when he is in contention over the last few holes, he has to adjust his clubbing to counter the effect of the extra adrenalin which is making him hit the ball farther than usual. Some exceptional golfers, such as Jack Nicklaus, welcome the nervous quickening of the pulse which accompanies a rise in emotional level, because it is only then that he can subdue his natural conservatism and aim uninhibitedly for the flag or bring himself to play a high-risk shot. A hint of this emotional charge may

help in golf but just enough to keep the player alert. Ideally he should be in a state of cold, calculating calm, for this will enhance both his thinking and his shot-making.

How, you may ask, can a player prevent the natural process of becoming excited during times of tension? It is something which happens of its own volition, like the contraction of the iris in response to bright light. In fact, there are ways of combating this process and once again it involves the adoption of sensible golfing habits. It is now, for instance, that the standard drill for setting up to the ball really pays off, because the player who has schooled himself into a set routine enjoys a huge advantage over the player with a haphazard approach to golf. But, much more than that, a golfer can regulate his play most effectively by committing himself to a policy of making the game easy for himself.

Short par-4s provide the best illustration of the value of making the game easy. A hole in the 300-yard range often shows the art of the architect at its best because the golfer is the victim of extreme temptation. If I can get away a good drive, he tells himself, I will have only a little chip or pitch to the flag and a terrific chance for a birdie. That, of course, is the very message that the architect has intended to convey; it is the tasty bait which he has provided to prompt you into rashness and danger. If he has done his work well, and made this birdie prospect inviting enough while subtly obscuring the perils, then the unthinking golfer will be severely punished unless his drive is perfect and finds its treacherously small target area.

Mark McNulty is a prolific winner not because he hits more great shots than the others, but because he makes fewer mistakes. If you want to be a winner play safe and be sure to keep your ball in play

However, the architect's cunning can be defused by the simple expedient of asking: 'What is the easiest way to play this hole?' Grief awaits the golfer who asks, 'How would Severiano Ballesteros tackle this hole?' or, 'What is the "correct" way to play this hole?' Avoid the kind of thinking which equates length with clubbing, looking at the yardage and automatically assuming that 300 yards means a drive-and-flick hole. Ask yourself what is the easiest way to play this hole and you might come up with the answer: well, it would be virtually impossible for me to reach any trouble or to miss the fairway with my 5-iron, and then I shall have a smooth 7-iron shot to the green and that will also be a doddle.

By this process the player has outwitted the architect and excluded the possibility of a disaster. He has also eliminated any danger of over-reaching himself, or pressing for extra distance with the tee-shot. For all practical purposes the hazards have been removed from the hole because they have been removed from his mind. He thus plays the shots in a state of mental tranquillity, with no fear and tension and with the utmost confidence. He is now a prime candidate for the state of golfing grace, a sublime condition which is achieved by a process of escalation. Because he is confident about that 5-iron he hits a good shot and that in turn increases his confidence for the 7-iron approach and produces an even better shot. His confidence increases with beneficial results in the putt which drops for a birdie. He is now on the upward spiral of confidence begetting better shots and thereby begetting more confidence.

The spiral of form also operates in the reverse direction, of course. Suppose in this instance that the player had used his driver and the ball had finished at the bottom of a deep pot bunker. He now curses himself for his foolishness and despairs at the prospect of a desperate sand shot. Confidence drains away and he is doubly handicapped, facing difficult shots in a mental state which guarantees that he will make poor strokes.

This strategy of seeking the easy way should

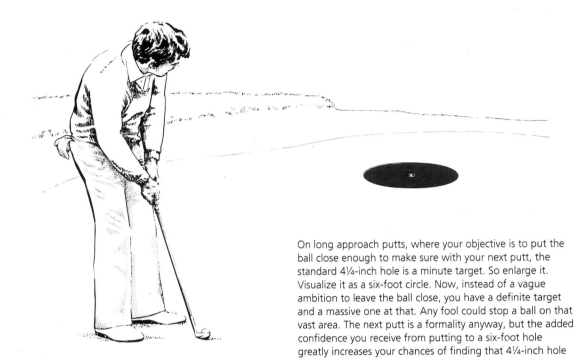

On long approach putts, where your objective is to put the ball close enough to make sure with your next putt, the standard 4¼-inch hole is a minute target. So enlarge it. Visualize it as a six-foot circle. Now, instead of a vague ambition to leave the ball close, you have a definite target and a massive one at that. Any fool could stop a ball on that vast area. The next putt is a formality anyway, but the added confidence you receive from putting to a six-foot hole greatly increases your chances of finding that 4¼-inch hole

guide the golfer on every hole and every stroke. Do not fall into the trap of persuading yourself that if you pull off a wonder shot then the *next* stroke will be easy. The most important shot in golf is the one you are playing *now* and that is the one you must make as easy as possible. Say you have a long putt across a tricky slope. Your instinct tells you that it is a desperately difficult putt. What you must do is neutralize those misgivings emanating from your instincts.

Turn it into an easy putt by mentally drawing a circle with a 3-foot radius around the hole and limit your objective to stopping the ball within that circle. There is no difficulty about that. Instead of drawing a bead on a tiny target with a rifle you are now blasting away at a barn door with a shot gun. Of course you can hit a 6-foot wide circle with your putter; it is a totally different proposition from finding a circle 4¼ inches in diameter. By this

simple con trick on yourself your confidence goes right up, making the task of putting that much easier and producing a stroke which is that much better and resulting in a putt which is that much more likely to find the hole.

Confidence

Confidence is the absolute key to golf. If you play with the assurance of success then you will indeed enjoy success. Forget all those ideas about fighting the good fight with all your might and giving 110 per cent effort. Just as the most effective swing is relaxed and languid and throttled down to ninety per cent of your power, so the most effective mental state is relaxed and languid and throttled down. Let the others go for the difficult shots and destroy themselves in the process. Pick the soft options and choose the shots you know you can produce without thinking about them. Then play them without thinking about how to play them. Just let them happen. Do not worry if your friends call you a chicken golfer. Just crow like a rooster when you collect the bets. There will be plenty of times when the state of play will force you to adopt a more aggressive approach. It will be time enough for heroics when you have no choice in the matter.

Concentration

The modern golf ball has been developed very nearly to the limit of its potential. In any case, there are legal restrictions on making balls which fly further than the present generation. There is some scope for improving the matching of golf clubs, both to the golfer and to each other, but these advances will help us hit the ball more consistently, not farther. Even if the legal limitations on the ball were to be removed, it would not be possible to repeal the laws of nature, so we can assert with absolute confidence that, unless a new breed of super-humans comes along, the golfers a hundred years from now will not hit the ball greater distances than we do. In the words of the song 'they've gone about as fur as they kin go.'

Even so, the standard of golf will rise. Scores will come down, partly as a result of greenkeeping improvements which will give the players better conditions to control the ball, but mostly because of techniques to control the mind. That is where the next great advance in playing standards will take place. And the specific function of the mind which will bring about these improvements will be the ability to fall into a state of total concentration as easily as turning on a switch.

The first point to clear up is a common misunderstanding about what is meant by concentration. It is *not* the feverish brain-cudgelling of the student who is trying to implant the dates of the kings and queens of England into his memory on the eve of an exam. It is *not* a state of mind which you force on yourself. The concentration we want for golf is the state of mind which we fall into when we are reading a fascinating book, or when we become totally absorbed in a television programme. On those occasions we talk about 'losing ourselves'; if anyone speaks to us we do not hear them and when we are forcibly brought back down to earth by a shout or a shake, we jump, as if woken from sleep. That is the concentration needed for golf: to become so absorbed in the game that we become isolated from everything else around us, enclosed in a cocoon of concentration.

Byron Nelson achieved this state of grace in 1945 when he won eleven consecutive tournaments and finished the season with eighteen victories. Ask him about technical details of his play during that year, such as how far he took the putter back from the ball, and he cannot tell you. In his absorbed state he was concentrating so well on the shots that he was unaware of how he was performing the strokes.

Johnny Miller was the same in 1973 at Oakmont, one of the most difficult golf courses in the United States, when he scored 63 in the last round to win the US Open Championship. To the spectators Miller had almost the appearance of a zombie. Miller was lost in his private world, insulated from all distractions inside his cocoon of concentration. Jack Nicklaus and Severiano Ballesteros are two other golfers who achieve good concentration.

Everyone who has played golf for some time has had what may well have seemed like supernatural experiences. You walk on to a green, look at your ball and suddenly *know* that your putt will drop into the hole. The outcome is preordained; tapping the ball with your putter is a formality and you do not even think about what you are doing or how you are doing it. The same thing happens with the other clubs. You survey the shot, look at the ball and the shot is as good as played before you take a club from your bag. Some insistent instinct makes you take, say, your 5-iron. The yardage is immaterial because you know that the 5-iron is the club for the job and the club swings itself. You marvel at the outcome as the ball plummets down by the flag, all the more so because from this distance you have always needed a 4-wood. Magic.

It seems inexplicable. In fact, it can be explained very easily: the shot was the fruit of perfect concentration. You allowed your mind and body to perform their task without interference from your rational mind. In those cases the state of perfect concentration was achieved by accident and you tell yourself that it would be wonderful if it happened on every shot. Well, if we can master the trick of losing ourselves in total concentration, then it will happen every time. What a prize awaits the golfer who can achieve complete control over his power of concentration.

Well, there are several ways of improving concentration. The first thing to do is enlist all the stratagems of Cunning and Confidence. Work out the easiest way to play a hole and pick precise targets which are well within your capacity. That eliminates doubt and worry for a start. You can trust your swing to perform its job because you are not putting any strain on it. By picking out specific target areas you are eliminating two of the commonest faults in golf thinking: a general hysteria that 'I must make a birdie on this hole' and a woolly-minded attitude whereby a player hits a shot without knowing exactly what he is trying to achieve.

What is needed is for the golfer to assess the situation thoroughly and then, as it were, to switch over to automatic pilot to perform the stroke. Your automatic pilot cannot do its job unless you have specified exactly what you want to be done. This process of programming the automatic pilot must not be in the form of giving it orders: 'Watch those bunkers', 'Mind that tree,' 'Don't forget to keep the left arm straight'. Nor must it be a sloppy generalization like 'Just rip it as far as you can down the middle'. The plan must be to use your eyes and ears and instincts to marshal all the relevant information and present it to your subconscious mind without comment or advice or warnings. In his book *The Inner Game of Golf*, the sports pyschologist Timothy Gallwey puts it like this:
'If the game of golf has to do with the controlling of a ball and a club with a body, and we understand that better control is accomplished by increasing awareness, then the priorities for one's attention are narrowed to the ball, the club, the body, the course, and the target. Since the course, target and ball (before contact) are immobile, they do not require the greatest concentration of the player's mind. Nevertheless, they should be observed, but not in a judgmental way. Your lie is not 'bad' nor are the lake and the OB posts; nor are the trees you went into on your last round. Neither are they good. They are best observed without attributing positive or negative values to them. Your lie is the way it is; in a divot, in the rough, buried in the sand or sitting up smartly in the fairway. It's important to see the situation in clear detail, and judging it either negatively or positively will warp your ability to see this detail clearly. Negative judgments tend to obscure your vision of what you wish wasn't there, and to cause doubt and tightening. Positive judgements tend to make you feel it's unnecessary to see details, and you become too casual.'
That is all excellent advice, but in one situation you may permit yourself to introduce a small judgment about whether something is good or bad. You will have noticed in professional tournaments that many players after lining up their putts walk to the hole and peer into it. They are studying detail, as Gallwey suggests, and in this case it is to notice the nap, or grain, around the hole. Often it can best be judged by seeing how the grass lies on the rim of

Few instructors would advise copying Eamonn Darcy's very personal action. But everyone would do well to copy Darcy's attitude. Golf should be enjoyable and he enjoys every minute on the course

the cup. But Gary Player, and some others, bend down low and the last image they have in their minds as they return to the ball is of a vast bucket of a hole. Your automatic pilot will not become confused by the little white lie when you make this suggestion that a 4¼-inch hole is twice the size.

The art of concentration is not a gift of nature, like a sense of humour, which you either have or you don't. You can practise it and improve it, by the process of making yourself aware of all the relevant details of the shot to be played and then losing yourself in the execution of the stroke, switching off your conscious mind and letting the swing just happen.

There is just one note of warning to be sounded. It can happen that you become so absorbed in what you are doing that you become oblivious to everything happening around you. That is fine, exactly what you want. But in golf there is one vital consideration which you must bear in mind; you have to remain aware of the golfers who are playing with you. The rules of etiquette do not mention it, but the most important rule of golf behaviour is to observe the flight and fall of the shots of your playing companions or opponents.

It is a courtesy, of course, to watch other balls so that you can say: 'Your ball is two yards in from the third fence post on the left.' But it is also a valuable swing aid. If others know that you are watching for the ball, then they can play their strokes with complete assurance and will not be tempted into one of the worst faults of golf, looking up before contact is made. That assurance will be invaluable to you too, if they watch your ball so the benefits are reciprocal. The best way, if you can achieve this trick, is to follow the example of Lee Trevino. He remains vividly alert to all about him, cracking jokes with spectators and chatting to his playing companions, but as he approaches his own ball when it is his turn to play he withdraws into himself, enclosing himself in his sealed world where he is alone with his clubs and his ball.

CHAPTER

6

PRACTICE

Regular practice ought to be a part, and an enjoyable part, of every golfer's life, just as it is an essential for tournament professionals whose livings depend upon it. For all too many golfers, practice consists of going to the practice ground or driving ranges and whaling the living daylights out of a bucket of balls. That session of trying to hit balls over the perimeter fence is one sure way of ruining your swing.

Keep Fit

Ideally, you should practise before every game of golf, but often that is not possible because there are no proper facilities or you do not have time. In that case it is wise to limber up with a couple of loosening exercises on the tee.

But when you do get a chance for a real practice session you should seize it and make the most of it, starting with your loosening-up exercises and then hitting some balls with the left hand only. Do not worry about distance; concentrate on making a clean contact with the ball and coming through each shot to a nice high finish. There are two beneficial results from this left-handed drill: you are strengthening the weaker hand and you are generating a smooth, relaxed rhythm. Next practise your balance by hitting some shots with the feet together. This will force you to keep a good balance and will remind your body to get its internal gyroscope in good working order.

You can now move on to regular golf shots, but do not be in too much of a hurry to start ripping off

those full-blooded drives. Easy does it. Start with the wedge and pitch to a target which is well within wedge distance. There are three purposes to practice: to tone the golfing muscles, to polish technique, and to acquire a smooth rhythm. And the greatest of these is rhythm. If there is a secret to golf that is it. Rhythm should be the first consideration on practice sessions and so the selection of the club is immaterial. Some gentle wedge shots to limber the muscles can be followed by a session with a medium iron for a series of full shots in which your prime purpose is to groove your rhythm. Only when you are swinging smoothly and sweetly should you move on to specific shot making. Now you can go back to the wedge and vary the routine. Hit a high one, followed by a low one (by keeping the hands in front of the club-head at impact). Be sure to follow your set-up drill with every shot. Resist the temptation to tee up the ball on an inviting tuffet. You will get some tight lies on the course, and this is the time to reassure yourself that a tight lie is not a tragedy. Of course, you can play from a tight lie, or a divot scrape. Hit down and through the ball into the turf and the ball will come up. Step on a ball and press it into the turf. Now play some of those and observe whether the ball goes as far as normal, whether it flies as high as normal. Make a game out of giving yourself difficult lies and seeing how close you can get the ball to your target. By doing this you will remove the fear from tight lies and will play them with assurance on the course.

It is not necessary to hit shots with every single club. Go through the odd numbers, reversing the

It is not always possible to warm up on the practice ground before playing but that is no reason for starting cold. It is necessary to limber up the muscles for golf, especially after a long car drive. This is a good way to work the kinks

And this one is an excellent follow-up exercise because it stretches some suppleness into the golfing muscles. From this position, with the club-head pointing down at where your ball would be, turn through a half circle until the grip is pointing at that spot

A weighted practice club is an excellent way for sedentary workers to keep their golfing muscles in trim for the weekend. A few swings a day works wonders. There is no need to have a special club for this purpose; any club with some lead wire wrapped around the hosel will do

Balance and rhythm. These are the virtues without which good golf is not possible. It makes sense, then, to practise them. Here are two exercises which I use to build my golf swing and they are excellent for focusing your mind on the essentials at the start of a practice session. Swinging a club with only the left hand imposes a languid rhythm. Do not try to belt the ball out of sight. Rhythm is the objective and a solid contact with the ball is all you should seek. Besides, this exercise strengthens the weaker hand, which is a bonus

Hitting shots with the feet together puts the emphasis very much on balance and it also helps rhythm. Once again, forget about world distance records. You should be trying to hit the ball *well*, not hard. That is the secret of long hitting, anyway

process to the even numbers on the next session so that you do not develop favourites. As you come to straight-faced clubs try some draws and fades, always playing to a specific target comfortably within your range. If you try a fade with a 5-iron and it does not come off, do not spend the entire session persevering until you make one move from left to right. Hit a straight one, then a draw. Now try the fade again. Your instincts will sort it out if you allow the process to happen without becoming obsessive about it.

Once you are hitting the ball well, think of the demanding shots on your golf course and superimpose an image of the hole on to the wide open practice ground. Imagine that a certain marker post represents the edge of a wood, or a pond, or whatever feature on your course has been giving you trouble. Now play the shot. It will be easy on the practice ground and it will be that much easier when you face the real challenge next time.

With the distance clubs, long irons and woods, dismiss thoughts of distance from your mind and concentrate solely on making a good contact with a lazy tempo and smooth rhythm. Remember you are not practising hitting the ball; you are practising golf. And golf consists of balance, tempo, rhythm, routine and thought. It is from these that all blessings flow and it is these that you should be practising. Think what you want to do with the ball before every shot. Mindless slogging is pointless.

Home

The best exercise for golf is golf, but that is easier said than done. The vast majority of golfers are lucky if they average a game a week and that is a very good reason for making the most of that weekly game. It is not just a question of pot-hunting, although there is no harm in being competitive if that turns you on, but self-respect and self-satisfaction are important to us all and we owe it to ourselves to get the most from our golf. Have you ever heard a golfer say, 'I played as well as I possibly could today, hitting every shot to the absolute limit of my ability?' No. By the same token, unless you habitually mix with the world's greatest champions, you have never heard anyone remark: 'I did absolutely everything I could think of to prepare myself for this game.'

You probably do not want golf to take over your whole life, but there are ways of improving your game at home by devoting only a few minutes each day to keeping your body and your swing in trim. For the over-forties, a few simple exercises when you get up in the morning will keep the back lissom and fifty swings with a weighted club each morning will do wonders in keeping those golfing muscles in tone.

An even better way is to get into the habit of performing the tyre drill which plays such an important part in the teaching of Henry Cotton. All you need is an old car tyre, a stick and your practice club with the training grip. Lay the tyre in a quiet corner and start with the stick. Set up to the tyre as if it were a golf ball and, holding the stick in the left hand, beat out a tattoo of back-handed taps against the tyre. Do ten taps, keeping the arm rigid and flipping the stick against the tyre with wrist action alone. Now do ten taps keeping the wrist stiff. Transfer the stick to the right hand and repeat these two exercises. With the right hand they will be the forehand taps, of course. In both cases hold the stick with the correct golfing grip. Next take your training club, holding it with a good grip, and do ten wristy taps, and ten stiff-armed taps with wrists firmly locked.

Do not overdo it at first. If you feel yourself getting tired, then stop and try again the next day. If you are feeling all right go on to half-swings. Keep the wrists firm, take the club-head back about 18 inches and whack it into the tyre as hard as you can. Really belt it. Sting it. Make the tyre jump. (You may have to trap the tyre against a convenient wall.) Now take ten full-blooded swings at the tyre, making sure that you have plenty of room to swing and are not going to shatter that priceless Ming vase. This is the one occasion in golf when you hit

Professional golfers spend lonely hours on this exercise in hotel bedrooms. Always provided that the carpet is true, it is an excellent way of grooving a putting stroke. By resting your head against the wall you eliminate any tendency to sway and the skirting board provides a valuable reference to judge the path of the swing

Plastic training balls are all very well for full shots in the garden but for chipping and pitching a regular ball is essential. That raises certain problems for indoor practice and the furniture should be arranged with some care before attempting this useful exercise. For the sake of domestic harmony and the antique Persian carpet, do remember to play every shot off a doormat

full out, pouring all your energy into smashing into the tyre. Imagine it is the boss/girl or boy-friend who jilted you/income tax inspector/hated politician (delete as applicable) and vent your spleen on the tyre.

Give this exercise a week at ten taps a go and then increase the dose to twenty taps for each exercise. If you do it properly you will suffer at first, believing that a steel band is being tightened around your upper body. Be of good faith, it is working. Persevere; you are honing your body into a formidable golfing machine. After a week of twenty taps you should be ready to move on to thirty. Then forty. When you work up to fifty, then keep it at that level. Fifty should be plenty to keep you in top-notch golfing trim.

Cotton advises his pupils to do contra-exercises as they go along, following each right-handed action with the reverse left-hand action on the other side of the tyre. This is to prevent your body from developing in a lopsided way. Whether or not this precaution is strictly necessary, it certainly will not do any harm.

Bad Weather

The difficulties caused by bad weather are created less by the conditions themselves than by our attitude to them. Let us start with high winds. If you go out to play with the attitude that good golf is impossible in a blasting wind, putting the par-4s out of range and making control of the golf ball more a matter of luck than judgment, then you are beaten before you begin and will certainly play badly. Welcome wind as an ally. Rub your hands with glee when it blows. Tell yourself: 'Wow, this will sort out the men from the boys. What a piece of luck. The other players will be blown all over the golf course, poor boobies, and I will have a huge advantage because I know how to handle wind shots.'

Just thinking along these positive lines will put you ahead of the game, but that brave claim need not be empty rhetoric because you can indeed learn to use the wind to your advantage. It is a prime axiom of golf that in order to make the ball go a long way you must hit it *well*, not hard. That applies doubly in wind because a well-struck ball is less affected by wind than a sloppy shot. Many instructors advise their pupils to swing easily in the wind, taking ample club and not trying to force the shot. Easily? If that implies reducing horsepower then you could soon start hitting sloppy shots. Swing *normally* and do not hesitate to make drastic adjustments in your usual clubbing.

When you are playing dead into the wind you should calculate one more club for every 5mph of wind. That means that when the wind is in your face at 20mph, a shot where you play a 7-iron in still air will need a 3-iron. Club golfers are reluctant to change gear to this extent. '3-iron? I can make it with a 5-iron.' Perhaps they can, by hooding the face and busting a gut, but even if they make the distance they are unlikely to keep the ball straight. It might balloon and be knocked sideways by the wind. More likely it will hook. But a normal 3-iron will hold its line and do the job with no strain, no sweat. There are no bonuses in golf for getting up with less club than your opponent, but there are penalties.

Forget about par. Par is a spurious, dangerous concept at the best of times. We would all play better golf if par had never been invented and we simply played the course as we found it, without any preconceived notions of how many strokes we ought to take on each hole. However, par does exist and golfers do get par-minded, so we must turn those facts to advantage.

When the weather is bad you should put yourself in a positive frame of mind by getting a card of the course and adjusting it before you play. You know which holes will be out of reach in two strokes, so adjust the par figures in every case. Now add any handicap strokes which are due to you, applying them to the holes where you receive them. A difficult par-4 played into the wind may now be transformed on your card into a par-6, offering you an excellent chance for a 'birdie'.

Let us say that there is an upwind par-4 which you have calculated will be out of reach in two

shots. You mark it par-5 and then *play it as a par-5*. Adjust your target areas, choosing a target area for the drive which is well within the capacity of your normal swing. Now select a target area for your second shot from which you calculate you will have the best approach to the flag. Suddenly, by a stroke of the pencil, you have turned the most difficult hole on the course into the easiest. Think of it as such. You will be astonished how often your pitch shot will finish close enough to the hole for a single putt when you play a hole in this frame of mind.

Cultivate that kind of thinking. When you find yourself in a position on the fairway where you feel that if you really caught the ball flush with the 3-wood, and hit your career-best shot, then you would reach the green, leave the 3-wood in the bag. Take your 4-iron and play for a safe position short of the green. That is the smart way of golf, specially when it is allied to the belief that with your outstanding short game it is a pound to a penny that you will get down in two more strokes, anyway. A 50-yard pitch plus one putt counts exactly the same as two putts.

Downwind shots are just as treacherous as upwind shots for the unwary. The temptation is to take maximum advantage of the following wind and go for the all-time record, so that for evermore you will be able to bore your friends with the claim that you hit the par-5 sixth with a drive and a mid-iron. They will be much more impressed if you play to your handicap on a rough day, so resist that temptation. Leave the driver in the bag and select your 3-wood, which should give your confidence an immediate boost. Select your target spot on the fairway without overdoing the greed, picking an area you know you can reach without strain. Make your normal swing. The extra loft will get the ball flying high and the wind will exert its full value, giving you every bit as long a tee-shot as if you had used the driver. On approach shots your aim should again be to get the ball flying high downwind.

Imagine that there is a high tree bang on your

Another Lee Trevino hint and a valuable one for playing shots downwind. You want to maximize the help of that following wind and, to do so, you have to get the ball flying high. Just imagine that there is a large tree on your line. Rip the ball over that tree and let the wind have a chance to exert its full benefit on the shot

target line and you have to hit a towering shot over it. Remember the paradox: hit *down*, with the club-head contact first the ball and then the turf, to get the ball up. Do not hit harder than usual, just the normal swing, with all your concentration on making a sweet, crisp contact.

Crosswind

The sensible golfer always chooses the easy shot and that applies particularly to crosswind shots. There is no point in trying to fight the wind. Even if you play a masterly draw to hold up your ball against a blasting left-to-right wind, you have absolutely no control over a sudden gust or lull as your ball is in flight. Either way your virtuosity will land you in a bunker. So aim off, allowing for the wind, and let it do the work for you. Of course, the ball is still at the mercy of gusts and lulls, but in this case there is something you can do about it. Study the area around the green and determine where the worst danger lies, and where is the optimum area for a chip to the flag if the worst comes to the worst. Plan your shot so that if a gust hits the ball it will leave you on the safe side of the green, and a lull will leave you on the putting surface. Or *vice versa*. The situation will be obvious if you analyse it in this way. This policy of nominating a safe side, either fairway or green, should be a regular habit, regardless of the weather. Bad golfers work on the assumption that the next shot is going to be perfect; good players know very well that perfect shots are rare. Ben Hogan reckoned that when he was playing at the very top of his form, and setting a course record, he might hit a maximum of five shots exactly the way he intended. Accept that some of your shots will stray off the line and be prepared for that eventuality on every stroke. Study the lie of the land and give yourself as much margin for error as you can, always looking out for the best escape routes. Picking a landing area for your drive close to a pond may be choosing the shortest route to the green, but it most certainly is

not the best route. Similarly, when the flagstick is set near to a hazard, a shot straight at the flag may be flashy but it is certainly not sensible. Plan for a 10-foot putt from the safe side of the hole.

All this may sound so obvious as to be not worth mentioning, but in that case there are not many sensible people playing in monthly medals in the nation's golf clubs. When you get into bad trouble it is often a salutary exercise to ask yourself exactly what you were trying to do when you made the stroke. 'Well I was trying to bend the ball around those trees and have it bounce through that narrow opening in front of the green and roll up to the flag. I know the lie was dodgy, but I had to take my driver because that was the only club which would give me enough distance.' Have you ever confessed to yourself that you were trying a shot like that? Ye gods! Even Severiano Ballesteros in an optimistic mood would not attempt such a shot.

Rain and cold also offer the sensible golfer a good opportunity to give himself an edge over the opposition. While the others are wet and chilled, and therefore miserable and discouraged, you can remain warm and dry with a little foresight.

With modern fabrics there is no need to be uncomfortable on the course. The trick is to trap your own body heat in warm air layers, and to do this, clothing must be loose, as it must be for a free swing, anyway. Thermal underwear under regular slacks, woollen shirt and sweater should be enough for the coldest day you are likely to encounter, provided that they are not tight and that you insulate the package with a windproof and waterproof suit.

The hands and head are major sources of heat loss, so provide yourself with suitable headgear which will keep you warm and dry and complement your personality. A pair of large mittens to wear between shots will keep the hands warm and maintain your feel on the club. An umbrella is often more trouble than it is worth but sometimes essential. Hold it with as light a grasp as you reasonably can. A fist clamped on the handle of an umbrella while you walk between shots can

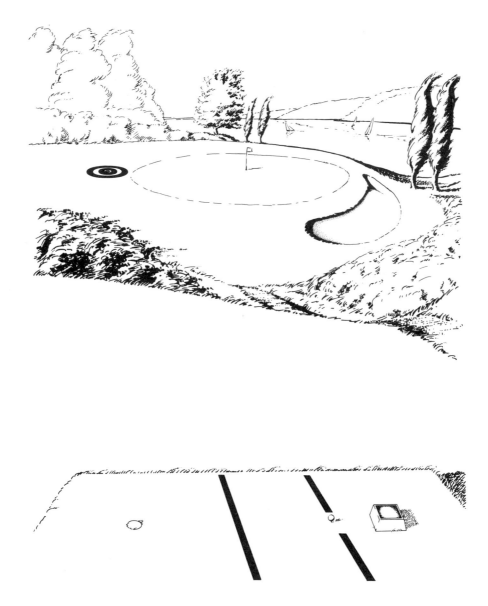

Why fight the wind? It is much easier to make the wind work for you. In this situation of a strong wind from the left, that bunker on the right of the green is an obvious danger for a shot played at the flag. There is no threat on the left so even if there is a sudden lull in the wind the ball will not find any trouble. So here we have an obvious target area. The wind will either blow the ball towards the flag or, at worst, two putts will be needed from the edge of the green for a safe par

deaden the feel in your hand. Always carry a towel and hang it from the tines inside the umbrella so that it will stay dry and serviceable.

If you wear a left-hand glove, carry a special wet glove for rainy days. Better still, do not become addicted to a glove in the first place. If you have a good swing, human skin will more than suffice to stand up to the wear and tear of golf, and over a golfing career you will more than save the price of a brand new set of clubs. While we are on the subject of golf wear, the most important item is a pair of strong, comfortable and waterproof golf shoes. If they are also light, then so much the better, especially for elderly golfers. Weight carried on the feet uses seven times more energy than the equivalent weight slung from the waist or shoulders.

Hand-warmers with slow-burning fuels are available and some golfers swear by them. If you care to carry a smouldering conflagration in your pocket then by all means do so, but make sure that you use it only to warm your hands. Under the rules you are not permitted to warm your balls artificially during play.

As for your shot-making in wet conditions, apart from a risk of splattering yourself with fragments of mud as you strike down and through the ball, the main effect of water is to reduce backspin on the ball and make it fly lower. It therefore has less bite on landing, although often enough the ground will be so mushy that the effect will be the same. Some makes of golf ball naturally fly higher than others, because of a different configuration in the dimple pattern, and if you have an important game to be played in soaking conditions it is a good idea to buy some 'high' balls from the pro.

In putting, steady rain will make the greens progressively slower and you must adjust your stroke accordingly. Always make a thorough inspection of the line of your putt in wet weather, no matter how impatient you may be to get the beastly business over quickly. If you detect standing water on the line you are entitled to move your ball to the nearest spot equidistant from the hole which gives you a water-free putt. This privilege applies only if your ball is on the green in the first place. If your ball is on the fringe then that intervening puddle is just your hard luck. It is virtually impossible to judge accurately how such a puddle will arrest the progress of your shot and it is usually wiser to accept that you cannot get down in one more stroke, and putt up clear of the puddle. A sure two putts are preferable to a possible three putts.

A puddle near the hole offers a rare opportunity to take positive advantage of the rules. You can putt or chip to the puddle in the sure knowledge that the water will stop your ball no matter how fast it is rolling. Now you are entitled to place your ball on a dry area equidistant from the hole for a sure tap-in.

Equipment

Clubs are a vital factor in golf but it is as well to bear in mind that they do not possess magical properties. You cannot buy a good golf game from the professional's shop. Extravagant advertising claims that such-and-such a putter will knock strokes off your handicap, or that a certain make of driver is guaranteed to give you an extra twenty yards of length, should be treated with suspicion, if not contempt. The ball cannot read the name of the famous player stamped on the back of your clubs, just as the ball is unimpressed by your bulging muscles, or your fancy two-tone golf shoes or your imperious commands to change direction in mid-air.

You are allowed a maximum of fourteen clubs, but this does not mean that fourteen clubs are necessary for the proper playing of golf. Until a golfer achieves a handicap in the low single figures he will be better off with fewer clubs and he will enjoy his golf more; his pleasure will be enhanced by the added attractions of innovation, playing half-shots and threequarter-shots, and his process of mastering the subtleties of stroke-making will be accelerated. In the whole history of the game only one man, Harry Vardon, won six Open Cham-

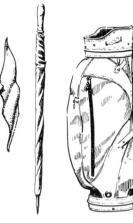

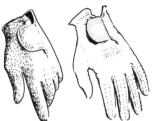

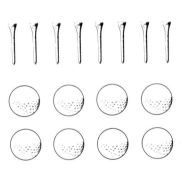

Be prepared. I am often astonished at the oddities which club golfers carry around in their bags. I think of my golf bag as a tool box and carry only the items needed for the job, no matter what the weather. Balls, pegs, pencil, pitch-repair fork and ball marker are obvious enough and the towel and umbrella are essential. I also have a supply of sticking plasters in case of scratches and a rule book which I always consult no matter how well I think I know the rules. I have at least one spare glove and a wet weather glove, and a showerproof suit. If it turns cold I am equipped to protect the two most important parts of a golfer: his brain (with a woolly hat) and his hands (with mittens)

pionships and he carried a set of seven clubs. Nobody before or since ever achieved a better control over the ball.

In assembling your set of clubs you should approach the task with the care of a sultan choosing recruits for his harem. Happiness requires that the clubs are in harmony with each other and in harmony with you. The first thing you have to establish is the character of your swing, and this is as individual as your fingerprints. Golfers come in all shapes and sizes, and height presents the first potential pitfall. A tall person should not automatically assume that he needs extra-long clubs; the length of clubs must be assessed on the distance from the hands to the ground when standing upright. Raymond Floyd and Bernhard Langer are roughly the same height, yet Langer has disproportionately long arms and can play with clubs slightly shorter than standard, while the short-armed Floyd has to have clubs an inch longer than standard.

The aim should be to have clubs of a length which will enable you to address the ball comfortably, with a tall and proud stance. If you have to stoop to reach the ball you will surely be laying up troubles for yourself, both in the quality of your play and in the form of excruciating backache. At the same time, do not be tempted to use clubs which are longer than you need, in the hope of getting extra distance. They will feel unwieldy and you will be unable to control them; you will hit the ball badly and lose both distance and accuracy. An experienced club professional is the best person to confirm your own conclusions about what length of club you should use.

On the subject of club professionals, they are human and are naturally keen to sell the stock they happen to have in the shop. However, if you make it quite plain from the outset that you are determined to acquire a set of clubs which is perfectly matched to you, and only you, with the same meticulous attention to your individual requirements as if you were being fitted with reading glasses, then you will find your pro to be an individual

counsellor. Once you have settled on the make of club you prefer he will see that the manufacturer provides a set to your exact specification. It may take a few weeks, but clubs represent your biggest single investment in the game and they will repay your initial care and patience.

Having settled the matter of length, you now need to know your optimum head-weight. Beware the danger of assuming that since you are a well-muscled hulk heavy clubs are for you. Golf does not work like that. It is not strength which governs distance but club-head *speed*, and that is the product of centrifugal force. We generate that force by a combination of turning the body and swinging the arms. Every golfer applies these sources of energy in different proportions. Golfers such as Sam Snead and Christy O'Connor are predominantly hand and arm players, or pure swingers. Jack Nicklaus and Lee Trevino apply more power through the muscles of the back as they turn through the shot. They can be characterized as hitters.

You need to know whether nature has made you a swinger or a hitter (it really is an arbitrary natural attribute, like having dark hair or fair) and the rough proportions of each element in your swing. The rule is that the higher proportion of hit in your swing, the heavier the clubs you should use. That may sound all very technical but do not despair, you can find out by a simple experiment. Get hold of a light club and some adhesive lead tape. Hit a dozen balls with it and measure their average distance, ignoring the obvious mis-hits. Repeat the exercise after adding ¼ oz of tape to the back of the club opposite the striking area, or sweet spot. Continue adding ¼-oz increments to the club and hitting balls, until you establish the club-head weight which gives you the maximum *controlled* distance. There will come a point where you are hitting balls further than with all the other head-weights but you are spraying the shots wildly; the weight you need is the one before that, the one where you were hitting balls far and straight.

You now have length and club-head weight (the

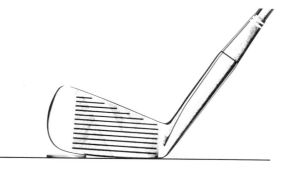

You can check the lie of your clubs by taking up the address position on a flat surface. The grounded club should show just a chink of daylight under the toe end, enough to accommodate a small coin. Do not check one club and assume that the others will be all right. Go right through the bag with this test. Any golf pro can adjust the lie of a club in a twinkling

gradations of weight and length for the other clubs in the set are calculated automatically) and you must now establish the best type of shaft for your swing. You must appreciate that the shaft does not of itself add anything to the shot; it does not kick the club-head into the ball with some mysterious form of stored-up energy as was once believed. What the shaft does is vitally affect the balance and feel of the club, and these qualities have to be harmonized with your swing, so that you can play every club with the same rhythm and tempo. The critical factor again is your individual mixture of swing and hit. That mix determines the point in the swing where the shaft bends, or flexes, and it is essential that this flexing is timed so that the club-face is square to your target line at impact.

It is possible to have your swing measured on an electronic device which will determine your optimum head-weight and shaft flex, but that science is in its infancy and once again the best way is to arrive at the answer by trial and error. Borrow clubs in your head-weight range with different shafts, from stiff to whippy. There are only four normal grades of whippiness and it should not be difficult to determine which is best for you. As a cross-check to your experiment, the heavier the club-head, the stiffer the shaft. However, although science can help the golfer he should never allow himself to become the slave of dynamic theory. In golf the rule which has the power of veto over all the laws of physics is that what works best for you is what you should use. Those supposedly intangible qualities of feel and balance can be reduced to scientific equations, but the proof of the pudding must always be in the eating.

Another vital, if often neglected, factor is the lie of the club. Hooks and slices may be caused by using clubs with unsuitable lies and have nothing to do with a faulty swing, and since it is a simple job for a golf professional to adjust the lie of a club there is no excuse for neglect of this point. If the angle between the shaft and the sole of the club is too wide, or 'flat' as it is called, then the toe of the club will dig into the turf at impact and cause a slice. Conversely, if the angle is too small, or upright, the heel of the club will dig in and cause a hook. You can check the lie of your clubs by standing at the address position on a flat surface. There should be just enough daylight under the toe end of the sole to allow a coin to be slid about a third of the way under the sole.

Another important factor is grip thickness. If

your grips are too thick for your fingers then your wrist and hand action will be restricted and you will have a tendency to push your shots out to the right. Too thin and your control of the club may suffer. Experiment. Get these things right. Goodness knows how many golfers are trying to correct faults in their swings when the error in fact is built into their equipment.

By now you should have a fair idea of the specifications to suit your swing. Do not be tempted to start your golfing life with a set of clubs which has been handed down from a relative, or given to you by a friend. Use them as part exchange against the clubs you determine that you need. Get your irons; only the 3, 5, 7 and 9 if you like. You can always fill in the gaps later. Do not try to go for broke and buy a complete 'matched' set of woods or irons; it is highly unlikely that all the woods, irons and wedges and the putter will be exactly right for you. Much better continue your quest with even more care, which is the way tournament golfers operate. Think of the irons as the infantry, the general duty footsloggers of your army. The driver, the fairway woods, the wedges and the putter are the special units and they must be perfectly adapted to you and to their highly specialized tasks. The driver and the putter are the shock troops which will take the brunt of the campaign and you must have total faith in them.

It may take years of searching, but once a tournament golfer finds a driver and putter to suit him, they become his most precious possessions and his truest friends. As with the sultan and his harem, the choice of a driver is often a matter of love at first sight. Keep your eyes open when you see a barrel of second-hand clubs in a professional's shop. Waggle them and if you pick one up which seems comfortable and natural in your hands then ask if you can try it. The pro will normally be willing to permit you to have a hit with an old club. Do not be put off by appearances; feeling is everything. Unless a wooden club is badly split it can be restored to beauty by the cosmetic surgery of the skilled club-maker.

The same goes for wedges, those commandos of the desperate emergency. They are the clubs which are going to bail you out of trouble, performing prodigies of turning bogeys into birdies, and they must be exquisite instruments of sensitivity. Beware of clubs which are proclaimed to be 'double-duty' for they will be unsuitable for either pitching or sand play. These are separate functions and call for separate implements, a deeper sole for sand (although not too much bounce, or the blade will be deflected upwards too steeply and catch the ball rather than skidding under it) and a gentler sole for work from the turf. Nobody can tell you that this particular wedge is the right club for you; we are dealing in the highly personal area of feeling and you must be the sole judge of the club which feels right in your hands and which performs right with the ball.

As your skill improves and your handicap falls you will become adept at marshalling your forces according to the weather and the type of course you are playing. On windy days you will want to carry a specialist driving iron to keep the ball low off the tee and for long approaches, and you will make room in the bag for it by discarding a lofted fairway wood (which might cause the ball to balloon in the wind).

So now you have another quest, for a 1- or 2-iron to serve such occasions. You find it like those fairway woods in the same pragmatic way that you choose a driver. The best and healthiest way of playing golf is to sling a carrying bag across your shoulder and walk; golf played from a motorized cart is not golf at all except for those who need one for medical reasons, and golf played with a hand trolley is often frustrating, apart from robbing your pulling hand of its sensitivity.

Until a golfer achieves a single figure handicap a suitable set of clubs might comprise: driver, 3-wood, 3, 5, 7, 9 irons, pitching wedge, sand wedge and putter. Do not despise the 5-wood or that specialized breed of highly lofted wooden clubs; they can be invaluable for long recovery shots from the rough because their heads are less apt to be turned as they come into contact with the clinging long grasses.

By the time you reach single figures you will surely want to increase your iron-club range to the full complement, although a 1-iron *and* a 2-iron is surely superfluous. Add one but not both and ring the changes among your long irons and fairway woods according to your assessment of what the day's golf requires. This process of pre-planning will help your play because it will focus your interest well in advance and help to achieve that desirable state of perfect concentration.

Finally, never bemoan your fate in having a shot which calls for a club you do not possess. Part of the challenge of this game is improvisation; if you do not have a 6-iron then grip down two inches lower on your 5-iron and play a 6-iron shot. During the course of a round of golf there will be numerous occasions when you will have to make minor adjustments and improvisations; it would be physically impossible to carry a specialist club for every shot you will be called upon to play. Golf is not a game of engineering; it is a test of skill and character. The clubs are tools and the playing of the game resides within the golfer himself.

RULES

Etiquette

Golf etiquette is nothing more nor less than common good manners. Any civilized person who bears in mind that there are other people on the golf course will automatically observe the rules of etiquette. He will not need to be told to play without delay, to wait until people in front are out of range, to invite the match behind to play through if a ball cannot be found, to leave the course as he found it by replacing divots, smoothing bunker sand and repairing pitch marks, to stand still and remain quiet while a nearby player is making his stroke, and never to shout no matter how strong the provocation.

Golf has 500 years (at least) of tradition as a game of trust played by honourable people. The golfer must be the arresting officer, and the judge and jury, for his own transgressions. Without honesty there is no game. The rules of golf are numerous and immensely complicated, almost the study of a lifetime for those who wish to become authorities on the game. They have to be comprehensive, covering every conceivable contingency, in order that the fiddlers and rule-ben-

ders can be brought to book. However, if the game is played in a spirit of true sportsmanship, thus guaranteeing that players will not seek to take unfair advantage, then the laws can be presented in a few, simple commandments. The first of these is: *thou shalt play the ball as it lies* (without touching so much as a grain of sand to make the shot easier for you).

How to Get the Right Rule and the Rule Right

Even if the rules of golf were crystal clear, which they are not by any means, occasions would arise when you would not be instantly sure of the correct procedure. The best policy is to carry a copy of the rules in your golf bag, inside a damp-proof container if possible, and to resolve the problem step by step in a logical manner. The first thing to do is to establish the precise nature of your predicament and this often involves reference to the Definitions. Is the ball in a hazard? Or out of bounds? Or on the green? The Definitions will tell you exactly how to determine borderline cases. Now you can turn to the appropriate rule, referring to the comprehensive index if necessary. Several rules may be involved. Take them one at a time. Work out the proper spot to drop from casual water and if your ball lands on a molehill, start again. The ball is back in play and you are now entitled to further relief. Take it. And if the ball now rolls into a pile of fresh grass cuttings piled for removal it is once more in play and you are entitled to further relief.

The real complications begin when you are playing 4-ball match-play and your partner commits a breach of rule, like accidentally playing a wrong ball. Does that mean that your partner is out of the hole or does your side lose the hole? Look it up. Don't guess. It is all there in that little book (Rule 30–3d in this case). Be wary about accepting rulings from opponents and fellow-competitors. If you follow a wrong procedure you will get no change out of the committee by pleading that your playing companion told you what to do. Confirm everything by finding it in black and white in the rule book.

On the Tee

Teeing grounds, or just plain tees, are delineated by two markers and the playing area consists of a rectangle two club lengths deep behind the line between the markers. It is not sensible to peg your ball at the foremost limit of the teeing ground, for two reasons. It puts you into an every-inch-counts frame of mind and encourages you to slam your hardest, instead of playing for a specific target area which you know to be within your capabilities. It also puts you at risk of rule 11, for if you play from outside the teeing ground you are penalized two strokes and you have to play again. In match-play, if you play from outside the teeing ground your opponent may ask you to play again. There is no penalty in that case, but the embarrassment of having to replay your shot, especially if you had nailed your first drive right up the middle, is often a severe penalty itself.

Teeing Ground

You are allowed to stand outside the teeing ground, provided your ball is within its proper limits, just as you are allowed to stand out of bounds to play a ball which is in bounds.

Ball Falling Off Tee

If your ball topples off its peg while you are getting ready to swing, or if your club-head nudges it off its peg while you are addressing it, or if it falls off while you are on the upswing and you stop in mid-swing, then there is no penalty and you can peg up your ball and start all over again. However, if the ball falls off its peg while you are on the down-swing then that counts as a stroke, whether you make contact with the ball or not. A stroke is defined as a forward movement (the rule actually means *downward* movement) of the club made with the intention of fairly striking at and moving the ball. So if you knock the ball off its peg while you are waggling the club at the address, or idly swishing the club to loosen up, then you have no intention of hitting the ball and it is not a stroke.

Improving Lie, Line or Stance

The golfer who accepts that he must play the ball as it lies, doing nothing to make the shot easier for himself, is unlikely to fall foul of the rules. It really comes down to a matter of attitude. For instance, if your ball is in a clump of thick grass, you may part the blades of grass to identify your ball provided you then restore the grass to its original condition. You have no divine right in golf to see your ball when you play a stroke. You can remove loose impediments and that is all. You must not bend or break anything fixed or growing, or flatten an inconvenient accumulation of sand or soil behind your ball (except on the teeing ground), or find a convenient stone to plonk down in the mud so that your foot will not slip.

Obviously there will be occasions when your ball is among bushes or trees, when you cannot take your stance without bending branches as you set yourself to the ball. Provided that you are *fairly* taking your stance, that is all right. But not putting your foot on an inconvenient bough, or tucking it behind your legs, or demolishing it with a practice swing. Just as you have no rights to a clear sight of your ball, you have no rights to a clear swing at it. This is the only rule of golf which invokes sportsmanship and your conscience must be your guide.

Unplayable Lie

The rules of golf recognize that in a cross-country game there will be times when a player's ball will find itself in a position where it is unplayable. A rule was therefore devised to get the player out of his predicament so that he could continue his round. It is the most benevolent rule in the game because the player does not have to prove that his ball is unplayable. There is no need to bully or cajole the referee. It is entirely up to the player. He can declare his ball unplayable any time he wishes, even if it is on the green, in a bunker or sitting pretty in the middle of the fairway. All he has to do is inform his marker or opponent that he is declaring his ball unplayable. Now he has a choice of three procedures:

1 He can lift and drop it anywhere within two club lengths of where it lay, but not nearer the hole; or

2 He can go back as far as he pleases, keeping the place whence it was lifted between him and the flagstick, and then drop it; or

3 He can go back to where he played his last shot and drop it there.

In every case he adds one penalty stroke to his score. This means that a golfer who plays a bad shot can always replay it, provided he is prepared to add that extra penalty stroke. Although this is a generous rule, its scope is not unlimited. If you declare your ball unplayable in a bunker you must drop it in the bunker.

Lost Ball

The universal remedy for all golf's problems is called 'stroke and distance', meaning that you can replay the previous shot by adding one penalty stroke. We have already discussed how you can apply this remedy at any time, under the unplayable ball rule, and it has to be used when your ball is lost. You go back, drop another ball (peg it up if the previous shot was made from the tee) and add a penalty stroke. The same procedure applies to a ball out of bounds.

You are allowed five minutes to search for a ball, starting from the moment when you arrive in its general vicinity and start hunting around. Check your watch when you arrive and call through the match behind. In order to save time, when your five minutes is nearly up you may leave your companions to continue the search while you walk back. If they find your ball while you are retracing your steps, and it is within your five minutes, then you continue with your original ball. But the moment you drop another ball it is in play and your original ball is abandoned, even though it may turn up within your five minutes.

In the case of playing another ball from the tee, it becomes the ball in play when you strike it, not when you put it on its peg.

Provisional Ball

To save time, when you have a pretty good idea that your ball will be lost, you may play another before you move forward to search. This is called a provisional ball. Now, if your search proves fruitless, you simply continue to play with that provisional ball and add a penalty stroke.

Playing a provisional ball is obviously a sensible and time-saving procedure, but there is one pitfall. The rules do not give you the choice between the provisional ball and your original ball, if it turns up. If the original ball is found then you must continue to play with it. Of course, it may be in a desperately difficult lie, say in the middle of a thick bush, and you feel you would prefer to abandon it and play on with the provisional ball. After all, you may tell yourself, this is only following the procedure for declaring it unplayable. But no, you cannot. If you decide to declare it unplayable then you must go back and play another ball. That provisional ball can only be brought into play if the original ball really is lost or out of bounds.

Bunkers

In the rules, bunkers are classified as hazards, along with water hazards and lateral water hazards, but it may be simpler to consider them separately. You are not allowed to test the surface and that means you may not ground your club behind the ball. You can remove obstructions (man-made objects), but you must not touch loose impediments (natural material) in hazards; they are supposed to be awful places and accumulations of leaves are all part of their hazardous nature.

Although you are under punishment, as it were, when your ball finishes in a bunker, there are certain privileges which you can claim. You may shuffle your feet in the sand to get a firm foothold. You may take your clubs into the bunker with you and drop the bag on the sand. More to the point, perhaps, you can take the rake in with you, but be sure to drop it nearby, rather than sticking it into the sand; that could be construed as testing the surface. You have all the usual rights to relief from casual water, ground-under-repair and to declaring your ball unplayable. In these cases you must drop your ball within the bunker when you take relief. However, with casual water and ground-

under-repair you have the further option of accepting a penalty stroke and dropping outside the bunker, keeping the spot where the ball lay between you and the flag-stick. If your ball is lost in casual water or ground-under-repair in a bunker, you can drop another ball in the bunker without penalty. Or you can take a penalty stroke and drop outside the bunker as described above. If you lose a ball in a bunker which is not affected by these special conditions then you follow the usual stroke-and-distance procedure.

After you have safely played out of the bunker you should smooth out your footprints and leave the bunker in the condition in which you would like to find it.

Identifying Ball

It is the responsibility of the player to ensure that he plays the right ball and the situation arises when you can see a ball, but you cannot see its markings. In that case you are allowed to lift it for identification, making sure that you call your opponent or marker over to confirm that you are not up to any hanky-panky by replacing it in a better lie. Since you are not taking relief you are not allowed to clean the ball, only wipe away enough mud or whatever to reveal its identifying marks. Then you have to place it back in exactly its original lie.

There is no penalty for playing a wrong ball from a hazard, so if you can see a ball you can play it safe in the knowledge that if it turns out to be a wrong ball then you can go back and play your ball. Maybe you cannot see any ball at all in the hazard. In that case you are allowed to brush aside just enough material (leaves, sand, etc.) to ascertain that there is *a* ball there, but you must not continue your excavations in order to reveal its identifying marks.

Water Hazards

Water hazards are places where you would normally expect to find water: the sea, lakes, ponds, rivers, streams, drainage ditches and canals, whether they happen to contain water or not. The usual lost ball rules do not apply to water hazards; there are special procedures and they are based on the point where the ball last crossed the margin of the hazard. So if your ball is headed for the water do not turn away in anguish groaning 'Why me? Why me?' Follow the flight of the ball closely and observe where it last crosses the edge of the hazard. You have a choice; either

1 Go back as far as you like behind the hazard, keeping that spot between you and the flag, and drop another ball, adding one penalty stroke. Or
2 Apply the stroke and distance remedy.

Sometimes there is nowhere to go behind the hazard. Say a stream runs right down the side of the fairway, or the ocean. In that case it may be designated a lateral water hazard (marked by red stakes or defined as such in the local rules). If so, you have a further option. You may drop a ball under penalty of one stroke within two club lengths of the margin of the hazard opposite the point where the ball last crossed the margin.

In both cases there must be reasonable evidence that the ball actually went into the hazard. It might be lost in a clump of grass outside the hazard. If you are in any doubt, then you must follow the regular lost ball procedure: stroke and distance.

Loose Impediments and Obstructions

Loose impediments are natural debris, such as leaves, twigs, stones and worm casts and, except in a bunker, they may be removed before you play your shot. Great care should be taken in moving loose impediments because if your ball moves

when you touch any impediment within a club length of the ball, then it will cost you a penalty stroke.

Obstructions are man-made articles and could be anything from a discarded cigarette packet to the greenkeeper's tractor. An obstruction may be removed before you play, and if in removing it your ball happens to move then you replace the ball on its original spot without penalty. Of course, some obstructions are impossible to move. You could hardly lift a tractor out of the way or uproot a telegraph pole. If the obstruction is immovable then you drop clear, after ensuring that your stance or the area of your intended swing would be affected. The fact that the obstruction is in your line of play is not of itself interference. The procedure is the same as for casual water and ground-under-repair. You determine the nearest point where you can make a swing without interference from the obstruction and then drop the ball within one club length of that spot, not nearer the hole.

Free Drops

It would be impossible to monitor every square inch of a golf course and remedy every temporary blemish, so the rules permit free relief from certain well-defined conditions, if the lie of your ball, or your stance, or the area of your swing is affected by them.

Casual water
This means puddles and slushy areas. The rule is that if you stand by your ball and water is visible around the soles of your shoes then this is casual water.

Ground-under-repair
This is generally ringed in paint, or marked, or defined in the local rules. It also includes material piled for removal by the green staff (grass mowings, leaves, etc.). If they have just been thrown into the bushes to rot they do not provide a valid

reason for relief.

Burrowing animals

Rabbit holes, mole hills and so on. The most important thing to remember in taking relief from these conditions is to determine the *nearest* point which avoids these conditions before lifting your ball. From that point you measure off *one* club length and drop your ball. It may be that if taking relief from, say, casual water on the fairway, this means you must drop in the rough. That's your bad luck. It can work the other way too, and there is nothing sneaky in dropping from the rough to the fairway if that is the nearest point of relief.

Remember: if you are taking relief under penalty (unplayable lie) you get two club lengths relief. If it is a free drop, you get only one club length. The one exception to that general rule is a *plugged ball*. This is when your ball remains embedded in its own pitchmark on the fairway (not the rough, or semi-rough, mind you). In this case you can lift and clean it and drop it *as near as possible* to the pitchmark, but not nearer the hole.

Dropping and Marking

You will get a reputation as a shady character unless you follow the correct procedures for dropping and marking your ball, even if you have no intention of taking an unfair advantage. It is just as easy to do these things the right way as it is to offend against the rules and conventions of the game, so we might as well get them right from the start.

Dropping

Stand erect, facing any direction you like, and drop the ball from your hand extended at shoulder height. If it hits any part of you before reaching the ground you must drop it again. (If it rolls against your foot *after* it has hit the ground then it is in play.) Provided that the ball does not roll nearer the hole than the spot where it originally lay, it may roll two club lengths away from the point where you dropped it and still be legally in play. If it rolls more than two club lengths you must drop it again. And if it still rolls outside the limit, as it well may on a slope, then you place it.

Marking

On the green, when you lift your ball the proper procedure is to place a small coin or ball-marker directly *behind* the ball (not to one side, or in front). Now, when you replace the ball, you must be meticulous in observing that it goes back on to its exact spot before lifting your marker.

Substituting and Cleaning the Ball

You are entitled to clean your ball whenever you take relief under the rules, whether under penalty or in cases of free relief, and you can also clean your ball before every putt. However,, when you are not on the green and your ball lies so close to somebody else's that it might interfere with his shot, he is entitled to ask you to mark it and lift it. In that case you must not clean your ball.

A recent change of rule has tightened up the regulations for replacing a ball which becomes unfit for play during the play of a hole. The intention of this change is to make sure that a ball is really unfit for play, not just scuffed or marked. You can replace your ball as often as you like between holes.

Moving Ball Stopped or Deflected

'Outside agencies' are people, animals or objects which are not directly concerned with your match, or your side in stroke-play. If your moving ball is stopped or deflected by an outside agency, then that is what is called a rub of the green and you must play it where it lies.

In stroke-play, if you or your partner or your caddies or your equipment stop or deflect your moving ball, then you are penalized two strokes and the ball must be played as it lies. In match-play if you or anybody or anything on your side stops or deflects your moving ball, then you lose the hole. If your ball is stopped or deflected by the opponents or their equipment then there is no penalty. You have the option of playing the ball as it lies or replaying the stroke.

Stationary Ball Moved

A more common occurrence is for a ball at rest to be moved. If it is moved by an outside agency there is no penalty and the ball must be replaced. The same applies if anyone who is not on your side moves your ball during a search. However, if you or anyone on your side moves your ball, accidentally or deliberately, you must replace the ball and add a penalty stroke. In match-play, if your ball is moved by anybody or anything on your opponent's side, except during a search, the opponent suffers a penalty stroke. You replace your ball.

Wrong Ball

We have already established that there is no penalty for playing a wrong ball in a hazard; you simply ignore any strokes and penalties with a wrong ball. Elsewhere, however, it is an expensive business and golfers should get into the habit of making positive identification of the ball before every shot as a matter of routine.

In match-play, the penalty is loss of hole for playing a wrong ball. What often happens is that competitors inadvertently play each other's balls. In that case the first player to play a wrong ball loses the hole and if you cannot be sure when the exchange took place and who hit the wrong ball first, then you have no choice but to play out the hole with the wrong balls.

In stroke-play the penalty, as usual, is two strokes. Obviously, if the wrong ball belongs to a fellow-competitor he places a ball on the appropriate spot. Note that this ball is not dropped. This case is exactly the same as lifting a ball because it is interfering with someone else's stroke and the intention must be to put it back in the identical lie, hence placing rather than dropping. You drop a ball to put it into play, you place to restore a ball which has never been out of play.

If you discover after you hole out that you have been playing a wrong ball, you can rectify the error provided you have not made a stroke on the next hole. What you do is retrace your steps and find your proper ball, add two penalty strokes and play out the hole. Ignore the strokes you had made with the wrong ball.

Ball Played from Wrong Place

Everyone at some time or other will take relief and then, after he has played his ball, will realize that he dropped the ball in the wrong place; or somebody else will point out that he has followed an incorrect procedure. If it is a minor mistake, involving a technicality and conferring no great advantage, then you simply penalize yourself two strokes and continue playing. However, you may have made a real bloomer, like dropping a ball outside a bunker when the rule called for it to be dropped in the hazard. In that case you follow the same procedure as for rectifying the mistake of playing a wrong ball. You go back, put a ball into play in the correct place and add two penalty strokes to your score. Again, you do not count the strokes made with the ball you played from a wrong place. After taking this remedial action you must report the facts to the committee straight after you finish the round. The committee will then decide whether you were justified in your actions and whether your score shall count.

The clear intention of this rule is to ensure that you complete the stipulated round according to the rules of golf and this is what you should consider in deciding whether to treat your mistake as a serious breach. If you follow the serious breach procedure to rectify a small mistake, like dropping a foot or so from the proper place, the committee, in the suspicious way of committees, may decide that you went back because you wanted a chance to play that shot again. The rules of golf never permit Mulligans.

The Green

You are allowed, indeed you are obliged, to repair pitch marks on the green and you should carry a little fork for that purpose. Always repair your own pitch mark by carefully lifting the indentation with your fork and then lightly tapping the surface flat with your putter. Also repair any other pitch marks you see, whether they are on your line or not. If you can do so without putting on a sanctimonious expression and remarking piously on the modern decline in golfing manners then so much the better. You may also repair old hole plugs, which tend to shrink in hot weather and subside. A handful of sand from the nearest bunker will usually be sufficient to pack the crevices. You may also remove loose impediments (sand, worm casts, hailstones, leaves, etc.) by picking them up or brushing them aside, using the hand. Do it gently. It is an offence to press anything down and if tufts of grass have been kicked up by the spikes of golf shoes, that is just your bad luck.

The Flagstick

For some reason which has neither historical nor golfing validity, it is an offence if a shot played on the green hits the flagstick. But we have to observe all the rules, even the silly ones, and before putting you have three options:

1 You may have the flagstick taken out of the hole (and either laid down very carefully well clear of the area of play so as not to damage the green or, better, on the fringe). Or
2 You can leave the flagstick in the hole and risk hitting it with your ball, thereby losing the hole or suffering two penalty strokes. Or
3 You may have it attended, meaning that you authorize someone to hold the flagstick in position and remove it after you have struck your putt.

When you are asked to attend the flag you should stand as far from the hole as you comfortably can and it is a courtesy to hold the actual flag securely so that its flapping does not distract the putter.

Always ease the flagstick in its socket as a precaution; it sometimes sticks, much to the attender's embarrassment and the player's chagrin, and a sharp tug can remove the hole-liner along with the flagstick.

When you play from *off the green* and your ball comes to rest against the flagstick you are allowed to remove the flagstick – gently does it and pull it straight up; no shenanigans of waggling it around to induce the ball to topple – and if the ball drops then you have holed out with your last stroke. To be holed, all of the ball must be below the level of the surface.

Normally in golf you are not allowed to place any mark on the ground to indicate the required direction for a blind shot, nor have anybody stand on that line, but you are entitled to have the flag held up to indicate the position of the hole.